THE PART-TIME
PARADOX

THE PART-TIME PARADOX

TIME NORMS, PROFESSIONAL LIVES, FAMILY, AND GENDER

Cynthia Fuchs Epstein, Carroll Seron,
Bonnie Oglensky, and Robert Sauté

Routledge
Taylor & Francis Group

LONDON AND NEW YORK

First published 1999 by Routledge

Published 2013 by Routledge
2 Park Square, Milton Park, Abingdon, Oxon OX14 4RN
711 Third Avenue, New York, NY, 10017, USA

Routledge is an imprint of the Taylor & Francis Group, an informa business

Library of Congress Cataloging-in-Publication Data

The part-time paradox: time norms, professional lives, family, and gender / Cynthia Fuchs Epstein . . . [et al.].
    p. cm.
    1. Part-time lawyers—United States. 2. Practice of law—United States.
I. Epstein, Cynthia Fuchs.
KF300.P37   1999
340'.023'73—dc21   98-20948
                                            CIP

ISBN 13: 978-0-415-92123-7 (hbk)
ISBN 13: 978-0-415-92124-4 (pbk)

TABLE OF CONTENTS

PART V
TECHNOLOGY 121

PART VI 131

PART VII
APPENDICES 137

ACKNOWLEDGMENTS

Many people, working part time and full time, have contributed to this book.

Qualitative research is a long and expensive process. We are grateful to the Alfred P. Sloan Foundation, which funded the major part of the study on which the book is based as part of its interest in work/family issues and the use of professional workers' skills. The study was developed through discussion with Hirsh Cohen, vice president of the Sloan Foundation, and Kathleen Christensen, program officer at the foundation, both of whom were of great assistance.

The book also drew on a study of lawyers in large corporate law firms, "Glass Ceilings and Open Doors: Women's Advancement in the Legal Profession," that was funded, in part, by the Association of the Bar of the City of New York. Its president, Barbara Paul Robinson, was extremely helpful to us in following through with this study. We also want to express great appreciation to the members of the Lawyers for the Advancement of Alternative Work Schedules (LAAWS Network) and its leadership, especially Jolie Schwab and Nora Plesent, for providing us with insight as well as the names of part-time attorneys to interview for this study.

We are also grateful for additional financial support for the study provided by grants from the Professional Staff Congress of the City University of New York.

The book was completed while one of its authors, Cynthia Fuchs Epstein, was a visiting professor at the Stanford Law School. We are grateful to Paul Brest, dean of the law school, for his generous provision of space, time, assistance, and an extraordinary intellectual atmosphere in which to complete the work. We are further indebted to Nancy Strausser, assistant to the dean, for her tangible and moral support; to the library staff, among them Andy Eisenberg, Dave Bridgman, Erika Wayne, and Paul Lomio, who not only tracked down source materials but came up with new ones; and to Carol Crane and Joy Nabi, who cheerfully and ably shepherded the manuscript through various revisions. Furthermore, the year at Stanford could not have come about without the encouragement and advocacy of David Rosenhan, professor of psychology and professor of law. He and Professor Mollie Rosenhan further opened doors to a most congenial scholarly community and circle of friends for this year. We also thank Epstein's Legal Profession seminar partner and longtime colleague, Deborah Rhode, professor of law, who stimulated thoughts about the dynamics, goals, and prospects of professional responsibility.

We wish to thank Martha Gever, whose analysis of time demands and part-time work in the Glass Ceiling study contributed to this analysis; and Elizabeth Wissinger, who was a research assistant on the part-time study and who contributed many ideas to it. Her contribution is especially noted for the chapter on the family. Robert K. Merton's hands-on editorial responses to an early version of our analysis of the social meaning of time (Chapter 3), and as always, his sociological vision, were of value beyond description.

We are also deeply grateful to Howard Epstein, who put aside his own writing and research to apply his considerable editing skills to the final version of the book, and whose intellectual power we have relied on for thinking about the small matters and broader issues.

And, we thank Heidi Freund, of Routledge, for appreciating the significance of our work and guiding it through publication.

We especially wish to thank the lawyers who participated in this study and who offered their thoughtful and reflective accounts of the experience of part-time work. In lives in which time is such a precious commodity, they were most generous in sharing theirs with us.

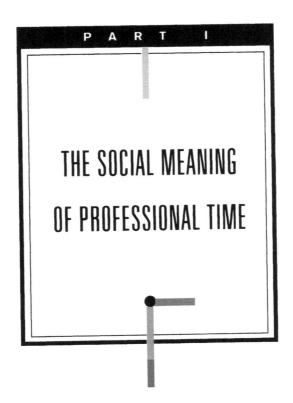

THE SOCIAL MEANING
OF PROFESSIONAL TIME

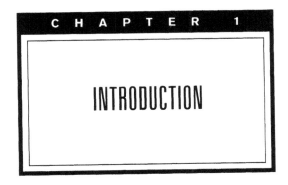

CHAPTER 1

INTRODUCTION

Trisha Wood, Hannah Kairys, and Leila Rubin Webb[1] are experienced attorneys who sought reduced work schedules to put a cap on escalating hourly schedules when their second babies came along. The three practice law in very different surroundings, but they share two goals that are important to them—to continue their careers as lawyers and to spend more time with their growing families. These goals increasingly had come into conflict as their careers advanced and time demands in the profession intensified, making it unlikely they could have "a life." Each was lucky enough to work in an organization that permitted attorneys a reduced schedule (and, of course, a reduced salary) and to have sympathetic supervisors who worked out schedules that met their and their organizations' needs. Though the new work arrangements did make it possible for the three to combine work and family life, they found that the solution to the family/work conflict incurred costs, many of them unanticipated. Little did they realize that there is a politics of time in professional life.

Although relatively few lawyers choose to work part-time, the observation that legal careers have increasingly entailed grueling pressures and the submission of every other aspect of lawyers' lives—home, children, and private pleasures—is no longer accepted without protest by a new generation of attorneys. These pressures and an antipathy to them exist among younger practitioners in other professions as well. The part-time option is drawing attention as one way to cope with discontent within the professions.

Working in three of the law profession's major sectors—private law partnerships, corporation legal departments, and government—Wood, Kairys, and Webb are among more than 100 lawyers who were interviewed extensively for a study devised to learn what happens to lawyers who turn to part-time work as a way of solving the conflict they face in managing careers, which seem to be ever more demanding of professionals' time at work, and at the same time reserving the time and energy needed to be loving and responsive parents. Wood now works four days a week "in-house," in her high-tech corporation's internal legal department. Kairys went on a five-day 9-to-6 schedule in a large corporate law firm—a law partnership specializing in legal work for corporations—where she is an eighth-year associate, a lawyer just beneath partnership in rank. Webb chose a three-day workweek in a federal agency office where she has worked for six years.

Part-time arrangements have served these three lawyers well in reconciling their work and family obligations. They like their schedules, are grateful to have them, and feel they are doing the right thing. But the solutions have brought some wide-ranging and unexpected problems. The women's careers are on hold. They face disapproval from colleagues who believe they "are neither fish nor fowl": not good lawyers or good mothers. Some of the lawyers they work with are envious, and some regard the part-time arrangement as an unfair burden on them. Kairys often finds that her 40-hour schedule—which would be regarded as full-time in most jobs—stretches until 9 or 10 o'clock at night when a high-profile case demands it, so that she works full-time or more for a part-time salary. The other two women have more predictable work lives with more defined time boundaries, but they are struggling to gain recognition for their skills and respect for their seniority.

An old tradition in the legal profession measures its practitioners' excellence and commitment not only by productivity and competence but by the number of hours logged and its visibility to colleagues and managers—that is part of the politics of time. The work arrangements of the three women are challenging this key part of the profession's traditional culture. They have become "time deviants"[2] who are flouting the time norms of professional life. Thus they have encountered the multiple social meanings of professional time, the way in which it is used symbolically to keep people in line or in "their place," to sift out those who would challenge norms.

Although they are socialized to expect long hours on the job, most lawyers today feel that they confront extraordinary pressures—unrelenting through the career life cycle and today marked by speed-ups and expectations they will work harder and longer hours. Furthermore, as parents of small children, many young lawyers also confront cultural expectations that they will be highly attentive to their children's psychological and physical needs, and be active participants in their children's social lives.

The realities of general workplace insecurity caused by economic downturns and competition, and the quickening pace of modern life—the ubiquitous use of the computer, multiple versions of the telephone and its appendages (*e.g.,* cellular phones, voice mail, call waiting, call forwarding, faxes), overnight mail, and car services (providing transportation for themselves and support staff at all hours of the night)—make lawyers accountable and available every minute of the day. The senior partner in Hannah Kairys's firm, Morris Steadman, complains that he is "pulling all-nighters" and works many weekends too. He told us, "I'm putting in as many hours now as I did when I was an associate coming through the ranks. The perception then was that partners didn't put in as much time as the associates, but today, partners as well as associates are putting in even more time." He said he would have been content to work full-time at his firm's old norm of 1,800 billable hours rather than the 2,300 he put in the last two years. His workday has stretched from eight or nine hours to 10 or more. But men rarely consider the possibility of a reduced work schedule; for them it seems impractical, and they know that male peers regard taking it for family reasons as illegitimate—sometimes as unmanly. And so it is mainly women who become part-time lawyers.

Unprecedented demands for availability and client service are now made on lawyers, and a tally of their billable hours is distributed to everyone within law firms. Henry Fine, a partner at a prosperous 800-lawyer firm where partners' incomes range beyond $1 million per year, told us that he does not look at the figures, but they were right at hand as he gestured at the charts on his desk that document every lawyer's output. Figures on billable hours are not merely known within firms, but are published in such legal media as *The American Lawyer,* creating invidious comparisons among firms. With such visibility of effort, attorneys working fewer average hours show up as time deviants, and stigmas attach to their part-time status. Such evaluation means that only a tiny proportion of attorneys—of either sex—will see part-time work as a positive and reasonable way to accommodate personal or family needs with career. Those lawyers who do practice part-time amount to just 2.6 percent of all lawyers (4.3 percent of associates and 1.3 percent of partners), although, according to a National Association for Law Placement (NALP) study, 92.2 percent of law offices report that they have part-time work policies (Lufkin, 1997).[3] The percentage for active part-timers also does not make a distinction between voluntary part-time lawyers and those who cannot find full-time employment.[4] Furthermore, part-time schedules were most available and most used in midsize firms, those with 101–250 lawyers.

However, part-time arrangements are being studied and observed by the profession's leaders and by managers and executives in the workplace because they are aware of pressures mounting around lifestyle issues, which have been placed on the agenda by the growing numbers of talented young women lawyers, who today are almost half of the newcomers to the profession, and 43 percent of the law students. If the current trends continue, women will constitute 27 percent of the profession by the year 2000 and 40 percent of the nation's lawyers by the second decade of the 21st century (Curran and Carson, 1994). Most of the women lawyers we have interviewed hold personal aspirations that include not only a useful and productive career but a healthy family life.

The trends we are seeing in the law are apparent also in professions such as medicine and accounting. The movement of women (including mothers)[5] into all professions and into the American workforce more generally in the last decade and a half, together with their involvement in ever more demanding careers, means that child-care concerns have become a major issue, putting the subject of flexible and part-time work schedules on the agenda of the professions. Furthermore, men also want to participate in family life more fully today and feel estranged by the all-encompassing demands of their work.[6] The model of the totally work-committed male career professional backed up by a wife who devotes herself solely to the family is no longer a viable one. Many male professionals are married to working women who cannot fully take over social and caretaking functions to free husbands for work-centered lives. Yet the role conflicts are still borne primarily by women professionals who feel buffeted by the often contradictory obligations of the workplace and the family.

Today, part-time arrangements in the law are theoretically available to attorneys who work in government agencies, general counsel offices in corporations, and in law firms.[7] But the form of the arrangements varies across these sectors, and the perception that it is legitimate to use them also varies. The negotiation and unfolding of part-time arrangements in government, corporations, or in private firms take place against the backdrop of very different histories and cultures within each of these sectors of legal practice. The large corporate firms clearly lead in demanding increasing numbers of hours. This is happening at the same time that women have achieved parity in recruitment—they now constitute more than 26 percent of lawyers in large firms (Epstein, [1981] 1993) and 37 percent of the non-partner associates in these firms. Though government agencies and corporate counsel offices do not require hourly commitments as great as those of large firms, the time norms of these large firms do pervade shared expectations and understandings throughout the profession. Practitioners in corporate legal practice in large private law firms, widely acknowledged as the elite of the profession (Goulden, 1971; Hoffman, 1973; Smigel, 1964) construct a "socially expected duration" (Merton, 1984) of time at work that is a standard for the entire profession. Attorneys in other organizations know how taxing work schedules are in these firms, either from personal experiences or from the war stories that circulate. The concept of the "full-time professional" defined by these taxing schedules is embedded in the very fabric of the legal work culture, and it shapes practitioners' expectations.

Part-time work is not a wholly new phenomenon in the legal profession. In the past, male attorneys near retirement often reduced their hours and were given the title of "of counsel." The change in title from partner to of counsel signified the downscaling of the lawyer's work to part time as well as the lawyer's reduced share in partnership income and in management of the firm. Like the position of professor emeritus in academic life, the of counsel title marked a gradual end to a legal career with a special status signifying success and respect from colleagues.

But today, professionals who negotiate fewer hours than their peers (or their "class") represent a problem for their organizations. They are *de facto* deviants from established guidelines for work time compensation, indicators of excellence and other practices believed to create profit for partners.[8] As in other realms of work,[9] when women choose part-time statuses they are viewed as double deviants, since their commitment is suspect anyway.

Thus, even as organizations appear to offer workplace flexibility, the employees who take advantage of it often face pointed criticism. In the invidious comparison with full-time lawyers, the part-timer is seen as less dedicated[10] and thus less professional.[11] This stigma reinforces the workaholic time ideals of most lawyers.

However, part-time status is not unmitigated woe. In the interviews done for the study that forms the basis of this book, lawyers' evaluations of part-time status run the gamut from acceptable to stigmatized. Though it is deviant by definition because so few lawyers work part-time, whether lawyers regard part-time status as legitimate or stigmatized depends on their work setting and on the attitudes of coworkers and supervisors who may have a range of views about work and family priorities, job security and advancement, and the impact of alternative work schedules on the organization.

Of course, these views and the cultural contexts in which they are embedded are undergoing change. Indeed, a study of part-time legal work provides a lens for examining and understanding the symbolic and functional meaning of work time in the professions, the impact of gender shift on the practice of law, the categorization of time in gendered terms, the role of new technologies, and the changing competitive cleavages among and within these legal sectors.

An Overview of This Research

The study on which this book is based was designed to determine the variety of experiences that lawyers in different types of law practice have had with part-time work and to analyze the meanings attached to the measurement of time for lawyers. We sought to understand the causes, consequences, and interpretation of part-time work in three major spheres in which lawyers are employed—private law firms (particularly large firms specializing in corporate legal work), in-house counsel offices in corporations, and government. Focused interviews were designed to permit us to examine the problems experienced by part-time lawyers in these different spheres of practice and to identify the obstacles and opportunities they encountered.

The negotiation and unfolding of part-time arrangements are shaped by very different histories and cultures in each of these sectors of legal practice.[12] Part-time work in government is regulated by bureaucratic rules and formal policies, but part-time arrangements in law firms and corporations are negotiated in cultures associated with more personalistic commitments and informal social networks. Because there are no rosters of part-time lawyers, and because some lawyers who work full-time had worked part-time in the past, we used a snowball sample to identify lawyers in large and small firms (including a few in medium-size firms), government agencies, and several large corporations. To develop the sample, contacts were made through the Association of the Bar of the City of New York's Lawyers for the Advancement of Alternative Work Schedules Network (hereafter referred to as the LAAWS Network) and through personal contacts. Other sources included interviews with attorneys from a study of eight large corporate law firms conducted by Epstein *et al.* (1995) for the Association of the Bar of the City of New York. A subset of the small practice sample came from Seron's study of lawyers in solo and small firms (1996). The federal government attorneys were contacted following a survey sent to their general counsels in the New York City regional area, and the corporation counsels from references by lawyers at large firms and personal contacts. Additional contacts were made through the division chief of a municipal agency. The total sample comprised interviews with 125 attorneys, including lawyers from 32 private firms, seven government agencies, and 12 corporations. We also used a survey, conducted by the LAAWS Network, of lawyers interested in part-time work (Schwab, 1994) or currently practicing as part-time lawyers, following up with lawyers who expressed interest in being interviewed.

All respondents were asked a series of open-ended questions focused on their reasons for choosing (or granting) alternative work schedules, the kinds of schedules arranged, the satisfactions and problems encountered with part-time work—including questions about the impact of part-time work on professional autonomy and quality of work assignments. We also inquired about respondents' use of technology, reactions of coworkers and supervisors, possible effects on career mobility, and how their family situations affected their choices. We asked how part-time arrangements worked practically, and what symbolic baggage they carried in terms of career ambition, professional commitment and family life. We also asked them and their full-time colleagues and supervisors about the consequences of employing part-time attorneys for their organization. A more detailed description of the sample may be found in Appendix A.

The following chapters explore these issues concerning the impact of part-time and alternative work schedules in the various sectors of the law:

Part I sets out the context of the changing legal environment in which lawyers work. This includes a sociological analysis of the meaning that time has for people in the profession, the norms this meaning generates about the necessity and importance of full-time work, and the way part-time work is regarded as deviant.

Part II examines how part-time work is stigmatized, the mechanisms by which this stigma is reinforced, and the way in which the stigma relates to gender. Further, it explores how part-time work entails negative evaluations of the person's work commitment. This section also analyzes the ways in which the economics of alternative work schedules is calculated by lawyers.

Part III explores the consequences of part-time work for careers in the legal profession. Issues of career mobility and immobility, job security and insecurity, problems of status incongruity, commitment, collegiality, and equity are addressed.

Part IV examines the ideological issues surrounding work and family and the practical problems that parents confront today. Desire for integration of work and family is commonly seen as the chief motivation for choosing part-time work. The family context, relationships between spouses, parent-child relations, feelings about the use of child-care providers, the division of labor in the family, including the "emotion-work" time division between women and men, and individuals' work-world priorities are considered in this section.

Part V explores the multiple consequences of new technologies on lawyers' lives. Echoing changes in the world of work at large, the law is also adapting to technological innovation. We explore how technology affects the pace and site of work, how lawyers' attitudes mediate its use, and how part-time work interacts with technological advances.

Three appendices follow: (A) on research methodology for the study; (B) on formal and informal personnel work schedule policies in various sectors of the law; and (C) tables on the attributes and characteristics of the sample.

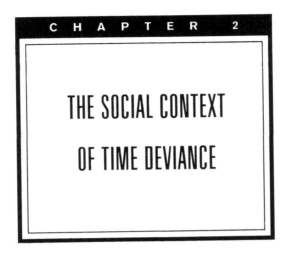

CHAPTER 2

THE SOCIAL CONTEXT OF TIME DEVIANCE

The Changing Profile of the Legal Profession

Although the number of lawyers who work reduced schedules is relatively small, the demand for work schedules that make it possible for individuals to have both careers and time with their children has become important in all professions.[13] The period of life in which any career is built coincides with the child-rearing years and thus many of the most critical professional passages—in law, promotion to partnership and to supervisory positions (Heinz and Laumann, 1982)—occur at the same time that law professionals are marrying and starting families. The average age of women in law today is 36, about seven years younger than their male colleagues (Curran and Carson, 1994). When the proportion of women in law (and in other professions) was relatively small, the demands posed by family and children were rarely, if ever, a topic of discussion. Professional men relied on homemaking wives to care for the home and children.[14] Today, however, the situation is markedly different. Not only are women lawyers worrying about how to manage both home and workplace demands, but many men are married to women who have their own work and career commitments and can no longer be solely responsible for child care and household responsibilities. Further, today's cultural views about bringing up children specify involvement by both parents, orienting men to be responsive to the issue of part-time work even if they would not consider taking it themselves (Hays, 1996).Younger people are also questioning the all-encompassing work commitments usually required in professional life, because careers are not as certain as they were in the past and they believe that a good life is one that integrates work and family (Newman, 1993).

The engine driving this discussion is certainly the workforce participation of women. In the legal profession, the representation of women has changed radically in recent years, as has the profession itself. And these changes reflect developments beyond the boundaries of the legal profession, in the society at large, with its shifting and often ambivalent views of work and the family.

The ending of a near-total rejection of women by law schools and law firms (Epstein, [1981] 1993) through litigation and changing norms opened opportunity and expanded women's interest in legal careers in the mid-1970s. From ghettoized positions in a few specialties and spheres such as government work and family practice, women now are distributed throughout the profession, working in everything from solo practices to firms with offices worldwide (Curran and Carson, 1994). In fact, the profile of women attorneys is closer to that of male attorneys than it has ever been.

In firms of more than 100 lawyers, the elite of the profession and a major source for our study, women now have numeric parity with men at the entry level. These large firms, moreover, have been growing radically in size for 20 years, creating many more openings for lawyers of both sexes. The 74,000 lawyers in these firms represent important banks such as Citibank and national and multinational corporations such as General Electric, Microsoft, Boeing, and Nike.These lawyers provide legal and financial advice to the commanding heights of the world economy. Because of their high pay and top-flight work, these firms lead the profession and attract some of the brightest and most ambitious lawyers in the country. According to Galanter and Palay (1992: 31), "The big firm establishes the standard for delivering complex services in the practice of law.The specialized boutique firm, the public-interest firm, the corporate legal departments—all model themselves on the style of practice developed in the large firm." Although women still confront "glass ceilings" near the top, they now are seen in the upper ranks of large firms. In 1980, 3 percent of all partners in large firms were women; as of 1996, 13.6 percent of all partners were women (Klein, 1996).[15] That growth has been unevenly distributed over the years. As law firm rates of growth began to contract during the late 1980s, the proportion of women making partner in large New York firms rose slightly; but their rate of increase declined,[16] in part because of continuing prejudice and in part because they decided to leave the harsh demands of large-firm practice. On the other hand, of the 3,685 partners made since 1991, 1,159, or 31.5 percent, have been women. Thus, while women have made important gains in private practice compared to other sectors of the profession, a look at the dark-suited male presence in any large firm's lawyers' dining room indicates the gender imbalance that is still typical within this sector (Dixon and Seron, 1995: 389).

In contrast to private law firms, government practice has long offered a relatively safe haven for women and for minority attorneys. Like male and female minority attorneys, women found jobs with government when they faced discrimination in the private sector. Local, state, and federal government agencies employ about 88,000 lawyers, one of every nine nationwide. Much more than private firms and corporations, government legal departments have personnel policies regulated by an elaborate bureaucratic rule structure. Some government attorneys are represented by labor unions, and many others work in settings in which a large percentage of workers are covered by collective bargaining agreements. In the past, government jobs available to women were limited, however, and they rarely were found in top echelons. For example, women rarely were employed in the offices of the district attorney and attorney general (Epstein, [1981] 1993). Today, however, they are a considerable presence in these offices as well as in the highest tiers of government service. As of 1991, 26 percent of lawyers practicing in government were women, and 12 percent of women lawyers hold government jobs compared with 7 percent of male attorneys (Curran and Carson, 1994). In our study, men and women were fairly evenly distributed among the offices of the various local government and federal agencies, making government one of the least sex-imbalanced arenas of legal practice.[17]

Women's integration into general counsel offices of large corporations is relatively recent, too. Corporate legal departments, like large law firms, have experienced considerable growth in the last 15 years (Galanter and Paley, 1991; Spangler, 1986). They account for 10 percent of all U.S. lawyers (71,022) (Curran and Carson, 1994). Located in the administrative headquarters of international businesses, they are frequently the sources of experimental policies addressing work and family issues. The growth of the law firms serving corporations provides these general counsel offices with a large pool of eligible recruits. There is a long and continuing tradition that corporate counsel offices hire their professional staff from among those associates passed over for partnership by the firms representing them (see *e.g.,* Galanter and Paley, 1991; Smigel, 1964). Many women choose to transfer to in-house positions in corporations because their hours conform more to a "normal" workday and are more predictable.

The expansion of in-house law staffs coincided with the change in the gender composition of law school graduates. Of course, men still occupy a majority of these positions; as of 1991, women held about 20 percent of all positions in general counsel offices (Curran and Carson, 1994), and they constituted 4.2 percent of top legal officers in the 250 largest corporations in the United States in 1992 (Epstein, [1981] 1993).

Glass Ceilings

Women continue to be disproportionately underrepresented at the upper levels of the legal profession. As the research by Epstein *et al.* (1995) on mobility in large corporate law firms demonstrates, the causes and consequences of this phenomenon are many and complex. Some ceilings confronted by women in the profession are imposed by firms through organizational decisions that make it more difficult for women to pass through the gates of promotion and partnership.[18] Some ceilings are a product of institutional cultures, old-boy networks that are inhospitable to the idea of women participating in executive committees; and some emanate from more overtly discriminatory behavior of decision-makers toward women. And some discrimination arises from the pervasive cultural stereotypes that still maintain "men are from Mars and women are from Venus," as a best-selling book (Gray, 1992) asserts.

Some ceilings, however, are imposed by women themselves. In response to conflicting pressures to perform professional work at high levels and to balance it with the demands of motherhood, some women make a choice to work at a slower pace, choose less demanding work, and seek defined schedules.[19] "Quality-of-life" concerns for lawyers of both sexes are currently being addressed in a study commissioned by the Association of the Bar of the City of New York, according to the *New York Law Journal* (Snider, 1998). And according to another American Bar Association poll, there was a 20 percent drop in satisfaction among partners at New York law firms between 1984 and 1990. Surveys on attorney job satisfaction by the *New York Law Journal*, Boston Bar Association, and the California Bar Commission on the future of the legal profession point to long hours and lack of autonomy among the reasons why more and more attorneys are unhappy (Ueda, 1998). The research aims to find out why there is a high attrition rate among associates, the younger ranks in corporate law firms. Such findings were no mystery to a woman associate at Wachtell, Lipton, Rosen and Katz, one of the major firms in New York, who chose to remain anonymous in the article. She was reported as saying there would always be "a fundamental conflict between a law firm that puts its clients first and having a life." Another Wachtell associate wistfully said, "I like my job, but I don't know how long I can keep it up." Women are often well aware of the implications of their choices, including the fact that they often are stepping off the track to advancement. Some express ambivalence when forced to choose, and others claim they never expected to be promoted to partnership; still others express anger at their firms and the partners who do not appreciate their predicament.

While it is typical for these lawyers to believe that their decisions are individual choices, they constitute patterns that should be examined and weighed in their social and cultural context.

New Technology

No discussion about context would be complete without consideration of a technological environment that creates time pressures as it simultaneously offers opportunity for work flexibility. In a book that reflects on the changes in law practice since the 1960s, Michael Trotter (1997) writes that lawyers once worked hard but at a slower pace. He recalls that plane travel was rarer, and many lawyers traveled by train if they traveled at all. Documents were type-written and copies were made on carbon paper or sent to the printer, making changes difficult and expensive—resulting in much shorter documents and briefs. There were no faxes or Federal Express or other rapid-delivery services except local couriers, and lawyers used the Postal Service, which guaranteed mail delivery in days, not hours. As we shall describe later, the development of various forms of technology changed all that, and it has had multiple conse-quences, both positive and negative. At the same time, technology helped to make lawyers' complicated roles possible by permitting them to conduct busi-ness while at home or elsewhere, and it also speeded the pace and rhythms of the work world. Technological innovations ranging from cellular telephones to portable computers that receive documents from around the world provide instant access to home bases, clients, and resources, speeding up turn-around time and eliminating breathing space between communications. In private practice particularly, lawyers' homes have duplicate equipment, and the market is growing for high-tech devices to make it possible for professionals to carry their "offices" with them. The catalogue in the pocket of any airline seat these days contains a rich assortment of phones and faxes and even attaché cases with built-in desks that can provide a portable work environment as one speeds through space.

Of course, technology cannot be isolated from such social factors as man-agerial receptivity and investment in it by both the legal workplace and the clients it serves (Zuboff, 1988).

Thus, the issue of part-time work must be seen as part of larger social change in professional settings and in general cultural norms and attitudes. It also must be analyzed in the context of the social meaning of time in profes-sional life, discussed in the next chapter.

C H A P T E R   3

TIME AND THE PRACTICES AND RITUALS OF THE LEGAL PROFESSION

A Sociological Perspective on Time

Society's views about the meaning of time—an important factor in the organization of personal and social life—form the backdrop to this study of part-time work in law. The legal profession, like other social groups, places values on the use of time, and lawyers have feelings about time that are socially patterned. As Lewis and Rose Laub Coser have written:

> Not only time reckoning, but also the way group members relate themselves to the past and future, *i.e.* their time perspective, is to a large extent dependent upon the group's structure and functions. Time perspective is an integral part of a society's values, and individuals orient their actions in the present and toward the future with reference to the groups whose values they share. (Coser and Coser, 1963: 639)

"The concept of... [time is] of special importance in the study of processes of social change...as an important variable in interpersonal relations and culturally patterned conduct" (647), the Cosers observed. This turns out to be particularly salient in our study of work schedules and the legal profession.

Although there are "only so many hours in a day," and how that day is apportioned among work time, family time, leisure time, and personal time (all socially constructed categories) can vary considerably, it also tends to conform to standards set by social writ. Time does not stand alone; it is always lodged in a *configuration in which other social factors are relevant. Today, we see that* time may be associated with, or defined within, the structures or cultural framework of class, gender, and race.Various groups often have different expectations about time and may be positioned differently with regard to their ability and desire to conform to time norms of specific culture.

Longstanding, deeply held, and tacit ideas about professional time may inhibit as well as open up the possibilities of part-time work among lawyers. In this study we explore the ways in which some norms governing time expectations reflect ideologies and sentiments about women's changing roles in the profession and the larger society.

Socially Expected Durations

Culturally created time constructs frame the ways in which time is apportioned in society. In the work world, such concepts as the "workday," "overtime," and "night shift" designate not only a time period but the attitude that should accompany it.Time constructs also incorporate expectations about the amount of time an individual should spend in the stages of his or her career and various life cycles (e.g., apprenticeship or retirement). Socially patterned expectations have been studied by prominent social scientists (Melbin, 1987; Merton, 1984; Zerubavel, 1981). In developing the concept of "socially expected durations," Robert K. Merton (1984) described the

> socially prescribed or collectively patterned expectations about temporal durations embedded in social structures of various kinds; for example, the length of time that individuals are permitted to occupy a given status (such as an office in an organization or membership in a group); the assumed probable durations of diverse kinds of social relationships (such as friendship or client relations); the widely anticipated longevity of individuals, groups and organizations. (265–266)

SEDs, as Merton acronymizes the term, apply to the "workweek," the "workday," and the "work life" ending in retirement as well as to the periods of time expected to be served before a worker climbs in the hierarchy (such as a seniority system in which workers are promoted on the basis of years in service) or otherwise attains markers that reward time spent in a work category (such as the watches some workers once received after 25 years in a company).

Temporal patterns of all kinds have particular salience for understanding professional work, in which time norms apply to stages of career as well as to everyday practice. Research on large law firms (Epstein, [1981] 1993; Epstein *et al.,* 1995; Nelson, 1988; Smigel, 1964) and small ones (Seron, 1996) indicates that time is a constant issue for the attorney. A shared professional culture shapes time norms and patterns time expectations, with consequences for the individual's rank, mobility, autonomy, and pace of work. In law, for example, there are socially expected durations that apply to the time (usually between eight and 10 years) lawyers must spend in an associate rank and fix the value of their contribution to the firm (measured in part by the number of billable hours they produce each year) before being reviewed for partnership; there are expectations about the time that should be spent in a specific job (such as a one- or two-year clerkship with a judge). Socially expected durations also apply to a lawyer's workday and workweek and to the lawyer's time availability to the client-professional relationship.

Most social roles have time expectations attached to them, and they may conflict with one another. Sometimes the expectations within a single role may conflict, for example, when availability to clients (see Zerubavel, 1981) is a time expectation that competes with the demands set by court schedules or with the need to attend to administrative duties in a firm. Or time expectations attached to a person's different roles may create competing time demands, for example, when an on-call lawyer must also care for an ailing parent.

The demands of contemporary private legal practice appear to create pressures for erasure of the boundary between work time and time outside of work. "Greedy institutions," a term coined by Lewis Coser (1974), describes the total, or near total, commitments demanded of members by organizations such as military and monastic orders. The term also applies to the elite professions.[20] Lewis and Rose Laub Coser (1974) have also described the family as a greedy institution, but with regard to women's roles within it, not men's.

The Professionalism Ideal: "Greedy Institutions" and the Social Control of Time Norms

Professional work typically entails workdays and workweeks that spill over into what others might regard as personal or "after-hours" time. Indeed, for the physician, lawyer, soldier, or minister, there has long been an expectation that they will not be clock watchers and will not allow competing demands from other spheres of life to undermine their professional work. Members of professions, ideally, develop a "deep, lifelong commitment to and identification with their work: it becomes a 'central life interest'" (Freidson, 1992).

What is the process by which this occurs? The profession's gatekeepers do not depend on the expectation that they will only draw recruits who are compulsive workaholics. When recruits become professionals they are exposed to the rules defining professional time, however informally drawn. The rules are learned and internalized because the individual "wants" to become a member of the professional class, and also because the rules are enforced by surveillance, as well as through the profession's system of rewards and punishments (Collinson & Collinson, 1997; Foucault, 1979).

Though not as absolute as the demands of "total institutions" such as asylums or monasteries (Goffman, 1961), the demands of greedy institutions such as law and medicine depend on internalized norms and informal institutional controls to ensure conformity. In the course of professional socialization (Merton, Reader, and Kendall, 1957), doctors and lawyers usually acquire motivation for hard and demanding work, and become embedded in a professional environment where devotion to task is rewarded by upward mobility while ordinary effort is punished with stagnation, diminished rank, or lesser remuneration.[21]

In law practice, as in occupations such as newspaper publishing or film production, long bursts of work activity extending through nights and often weekends are required to meet deadlines and to coordinate with the competing schedules of other participants in the enterprise. The normal mode of work is often a crisis mode. "A lot of corporate work tends to be crisis work, night and day," said George Klass, a seventh-year associate in a firm known for its mergers and acquisitions work.

Further, law firms and other legal workplaces constitute "occupational communities" (Goode, 1957) that foster a sense of a common identity and destiny (Pavalko, 1988). Shared norms and values reinforce a sense of common identity, and they control the behavior of members. Commitment is a reflection of the internalization of professional norms, and in both large and small law firms adherence to time norms is often both a symbolic and objective indicator of commitment. General identification as a legal professional is often translated into ties to a specific firm and its culture. Symbolically, lawyers identify with the firm by verbal references (*e.g.,* "my partners," and "my firm"). Thus, fulfilling time norms that specify not only hours of work but social time with colleagues at firms and private events marks professional assimilation for many lawyers.[22]

Commitment to clients is a further mandate for the professional. Because of the "service ideal" (Parsons, 1939 [1954]), professionals are responsive to clients both for economic reasons *and* because they feel obligated to be attentive; they are always on call. This is, of course, both ideological and practical. Managing partners in large firms express the practical side more and more today as intensified competition means they can no longer count on long-term relationships with clients (Epstein *et al.,* 1995; Linowitz with Mayer, 1994).

Mark Ahrens, a lawyer interviewed at a distinguished corporate law firm, spelled it out:

> This is a very competitive profession, and there are plenty of law firms that would like to have any one of our larger clients. If we can't service them or can't give them what they need at all levels, they'll give somebody else a shot. That's the way out in the world. That's the way of competition.
>
> •   •   •
>
> All of our clients have sizable in-house legal departments that do their more routine transactions, as well as have people available working for them that will do them. When they come to us, it's a big high-profile deal.... It needs to be done well and to be done fast.

Objectively measured, lawyers' work for specific clients is converted into billable hours. These hours, billed to each client, are the principal source of income to the firm. But they become a measure of commitment to the client and to the firm. They also serve as proxies for other, harder-to-observe attributes, such as ambition and commitment to a career.[23] Indeed, increasingly, associates at large firms equate success, promotion, and prestige with hours billed. Increased hours have become the norm.[24] The most competitive associates eager to win the partnership race against their peers therefore may not only accept a longer working day, but they may promote it (Kronman, 1993). Indeed, Landers, Rebitzer, and Taylor (1996) propose that it is common for large corporate law firms to settle into a "rat race" equilibrium in which attorneys are overworked.

Lawyers, like other high-ranking professionals, expect to be able to determine their schedules (Goode, 1957; Parsons, [1939] 1954). But they face structured ambivalence (Merton, 1976) when confronted with stringent work-hour norms and other symbolic baggage transforming hours worked into a proxy for the lawyer's commitment to his or her firm and career. Thus, the professional (as well as many other workers with high occupational statuses) is socialized to rationalize working hours far in excess of what has become a culturally normative American 40-hour workweek.[25] There are legitimate exceptions to the professional norm. For example, lawyers, like other professionals, may be able to delegate certain responsibilities and reduce their actual hours when they contribute to their organization in other ways; in law, this means bringing new business into the firm.

The socially expected duration of work for clients, precisely measured by billable hours of attorneys in large corporate law practices, evolves into an expectation about the suitable amount of time an associate should put in to be regarded as a worthwhile candidate for promotion.[26] As an associate, or even as a partner, logging "excessive" hours is regarded as a sign of machismo, a heroic activity. In law, where work may be evaluated both objectively (measured by cases won and value of deals closed), or subjectively (assessment of a person's "ideas"), hours worked serve as both objective and subjective evaluations, translating into a proxy for dedication and excellence.

Large-Firm Time Norms as the Standard in Other Legal Sectors

Practitioners in private corporate legal practice, widely acknowledged to be the elite of the profession (Goulden, 1971; Hoffman, 1973; Smigel, 1964),[27] construct the socially expected durations of time at work that become the standard for the entire profession. Whether the legal practice is in the corporate world or government, the notion of "full time" in large law firms is the social reference for all discussions of full-time and part-time work. Attorneys in other organizations know how taxing the work schedules are in these firms, either from personal experience or from stories that circulate.

It has been observed for some time (Smigel, 1964) that the more prestigious the firm, the more hours its lawyers are required to be "on duty" to respond to client needs. The net effect of these social pressures is reinforced by the expectation that "full time" means that lawyers are required to "always be on the job" for their clients (Zerubavel, 1981: 148). Full-time professional work means that lawyers are expected to "live, breathe, eat, and sleep" their work (Morrill, 1995: 38).[28]

Although there have always been mythic accounts of lawyers' dedication to their firms'[29] expectations for long work hours, demands for increasing numbers of billable hours have been reported widely in recent years (Epstein *et al.,* 1995). This demand, especially in large firms, to work ever increasing numbers of hours in billable activities, and the lack of time in both large and small firms for non-billable activities such as client development and administration, have led leaders of the legal profession to highlight the issue of time pressures (Bok, 1993; Kronman, 1993; Linowitz with Mayer, 1994) and researchers to give attention to the reasons for such time pressures and their consequences for the women and men in the profession (Gilson and Mnookin, 1989; Rebitzer and Taylor, 1995) as well as the ethos of the profession itself.[30]

Yet even in legal sectors where the time requirements are not as arduous, time norms prevail. Rituals of display (Goffman, 1959)[31] can be found in many parts of the profession, indicating commitment through long visible hours on the job, and deadlines that must coordinate with business conducted with large firms and with the court system.

Time as Social and Professional Capital

Lawyers' "human capital" (Gilson and Mnookin, 1985: 324) is the coin of their professional success. Their reputation for service and quality is a key component, along with training and experience in practicing law—skill, craft, and shrewdness; a passion for winning; and an attractive personal style.[32] A reputation for availability is also part of the attorney's "symbolic capital" (Bourdieu, [1972] 1977: 183). A lawyer's human and symbolic capital are purchased by clients and become mobilized in "service" to them.

Further, round-the-clock availability is no longer regarded as a gesture made only in cases of last-minute deadlines or emergencies—a theoretical promise of being "on duty" (Smigel, 1964) all the time. High-profile clients expect immediate and constant responsiveness, ostensibly to make competitive "deals" or to meet the challenges of opponents in litigation. Moreover, as markets globalize and technology expands, law firms are having to adjust to what are becoming the "normal demands" of international businesses, which operate 24 hours a day in time zones around the world.

Time for socializing is another form of currency the firm uses to engage clients and preserve good relations with them. As in the past, lawyers nurture new business contacts and reinforce ties to existing clients by fostering social relationships and entertaining them at dinner, sports events, and the theater, fusing work time with private time.

Large corporate firms, the pinnacle of the profession and its standard setter, choose lawyers who are believed to have the potential to acquire superior human and symbolic capital, or who already have demonstrated their possession of it. It is hoped that those who are selected as firm members will build the name of the firm and attract the high-prestige and top-dollar clients the firm relies on serving. Although in the past, client-firm relationships tended to be fairly constant over a period of years and the expectation was that they would be committed to each other through time, in today's competitive environment client loyalty must be won over and over again.[33]

Time Monitoring and Visibility

In addition to outside pressures, changes within law firms have intensified the focus on hours. Time has become objectified and more visible with stricter documentation of billable hours through computerized accounting systems (Gilson and Mnookin, 1989). Hours billed are also a part of the control system by which associates are assessed by managing partners; and even partners' hours may be observed by colleagues.[34] The number of hours is not, however, the only dimension of time monitoring.

When people work and *where* they work are also noticed and provide an overall cast to the social perception of a lawyer's time at work. As we shall see in the chapter on technology, work at home may have multiple consequences for lawyers; it permits flexibility, but it also removes the lawyer from visibility. Yet, some lawyers who seem to be working in the office may in fact be "at work" but not working all the time. Several lawyers interviewed for this study mentioned that, among associates especially, staying late at the office may be motivated more by a desire to appear hardworking than by the actual demands of an assignment or case. Consistent late-night work may also result from inefficient work habits, some attorneys say. Some associates faulted the managing skills of superiors for their problematic schedules; one lawyer reported that she went to the gym for several hours during the workday because she knew she would be pulling an "all-nighter."

Legacies of Professional Culture

Thus, norms defining the typical professional workday and workweek derive from multiple origins. They are shaped by client expectations, economic pressures, and traditions created and perpetuated by the older partners. As the sociologist Maurice Halbwachs ([1941, 1952] 1992) noted in his work on the social framework of memory, tradition is based on collective memory. Law, as well as other occupational communities, is bound by mystiques about the distinctive and unique feats performed by its members. In law, part of the mystique is communicated by stories about arduous and long hours on cases, tales that bolster a sense of professional community (164). Some stories come from partners' memories of their own experiences in the junior ranks and their recollections of how hard they worked; the memories become embedded in the law firm's control system, ensuring the productivity of new cohorts of lawyers. Mythic accounts abound, boasting of heroic endeavors on cases in which lawyers worked through many nights and weekends as well as on major holidays such as Thanksgiving and Christmas. Although lamented as arduous and terrible, a sense of honor adheres to those who have gone through the experience. There is also a hint of nostalgia for an idealized golden past (Gabriel, 1993) when men-only firms did not have to contend with the work/family conflicts that women attorneys brought and which many regard as superfluous "lifestyle" issues. These experiences become part of the institutional memory of firms, but they are selective memories in that they recollect a workday of long hours worked solely by men without domestic responsibilities.

Yet, time heroics were in the past regarded as appropriate to professional youth. As part of the socially expected duration of stages in a professional career, round-the-clock service was expected to ease off; senior partners in large firms looked to a time when advanced status would permit them to slow down and enjoy the fruits of years of dedicated labor. More recently, however, attorneys report that this perquisite of seniority is disappearing. As the demands of business development ("rainmaking") have increased and there is cutthroat competition among firms for clients, they explain, partners of all ranks are called on to continue to work at a very demanding pace.

Today, the legitimacy of the greedy institution is challenged by individuals' demands—especially by younger professionals—for balanced lives providing "quality time" with children, families, and friends and eschewing the patterns of the past.[35] Time has become a precious commodity, increasing in value perhaps even more than money (Goode, 1979).[36]

Thus, the traditional notion of full-time legal work is under attack by many practitioners. Some are demanding flexible or reduced work schedules, the possibility of working off-site (increasingly possible with the new technologies), or job sharing. This also comes at a time when the workplace itself is scrutinizing the efficiency and effectiveness of current practices, looking to alternative modes of organization to reduce waste, reduce hierarchies, and increase productivity. Yet, as we shall describe more fully, these pressures are competing with professional ideals of work, and the matter of what is an acceptable or preferable number of work hours has become "contested terrain" (Edwards, 1979).

We shall show in this book, however, that the contest is not a fair one. No matter where they work, most of the lawyers we studied who work fewer hours than their peers (or their "class") are *de facto* deviants from established guidelines for work time. They challenge the standard indicators of excellence and do not engage in practices believed to create much profit for their institutions (see, *e.g.*, Galanter and Palay, 1991). Even as organizations appear to grant these new demands, they define those who take them as deviants; only some part-timers avoid the stigma of difference. And, as in other realms of work,[37] because women's commitment to work has not been fully accepted, and because disproportionately they acquire part-time status, they face being defined as double deviants.

But time boundaries never stand still. They change conceptually and behaviorally and often are not synchronized, requiring difficult adjustments in the lives of individuals and in the social groups of which those individuals are a part. The following chapters describe the complex issues facing time deviants in law today.

PART II

CULTURAL PERSPECTIVES

ON PART-TIME WORK

AND ITS CONSEQUENCES

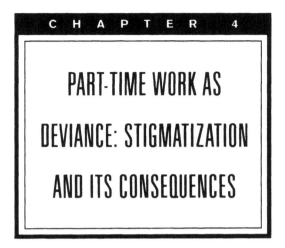

CHAPTER 4

PART-TIME WORK AS
DEVIANCE: STIGMATIZATION
AND ITS CONSEQUENCES

The image of the totally dedicated professional creates a sharp contrast with the image of the part-timer. In the invidious comparison with full-time lawyers, the part-timer is often seen as less dedicated and less professional—a "time deviant."

Our research found clear evidence that part-time lawyers are stigmatized. It also noted the function this stigma serves in reinforcing time ideals for the majority of lawyers. It led us to seek and ponder the conditions under which part-time attorneys are insulated from stigmatization.

Lawyers who take on part-time status learn they are stigmatized directly (*e.g.*, when they are taken off the track to partnership) or indirectly (*e.g.*, when they become the butt of jokes about their schedules). Some just feel "it's in the air." Arthur Kant, one of the few male lawyers we encountered who worked a reduced schedule, *anticipated* that he would be stigmatized for his part-time status later in his career even though he had not thus far drawn negative comments; he was well aware that the legal profession honors workaholism, and he expected to be punished for doing less.

We use the term "stigma" here in its sociological sense to convey the way in which "otherness" is determined by social definition—by labeling. This is played out in interaction, through understandings commonly shared and communicated by comments that carry messages regarding socially appropriate behavior. Stigma, as Erving Goffman (1963) pointed out, has to do with relationships, not attributes.[38] Stigma serves to place a boundary around the "normal." What is at issue is deviation from the norm.

Facing Stigma

The definition and enunciation of the stigma on part-time work as a deviation from the normal is captured by the comment of Georgia Lamm, a tenth-year associate in a large firm who felt she had to remove herself from a partnership track when her son was born but who nonetheless felt professionally committed:

> There are both explicit and implicit beliefs in law firms that the best lawyers don't have lives.... [A colleague] was told gratuitously in an elevator by a partner that she couldn't be serious about her work because she worked part-time. I am serious about my work. But not in the way he meant, which is totally single-minded with nothing else mattering.

And, as Leslie Reiff, a former part-time partner who recently had switched back to full-time work, reported, "The institutional perception of part time as bad can't be battled via policy—it's a mind-set among lawyers." August Covington White hoped to circumvent this mind-set by getting approval for a title as consulting tax counsel in a part-time job. As he jokingly commented: "Call it anything, but don't call it part-time!"

The mind-set seemed fairly clear to one of the authors of this book during a dinner party conversation with a noted professor at a major law school who also was a consultant for a major New York law firm. Describing this study, the author asked his opinion of the feasibility of part-time work in the New York firm. "Impossible," he asserted without hesitation. "But don't you work part-time for the firm?" she asked. "That's different," he said, "I provide expertise they need." "But couldn't a woman who wanted to limit her hours also provide expertise on a part-time basis as you do?" the questioner continued. "I don't think we are getting anywhere with this conversation," the professor snapped as he turned away, obviously irritated at being categorized as a "part-timer" rather than a "consultant."

Part-time lawyers are well aware of the different evaluations they are apt to confront both inside and outside the legal workplace. There are consequences for them personally, with regard to their self-images and their reputations.

The intensity of the stigma experienced by attorneys working part-time varies with the sector of the law in which they work (large law firms, corporations, or government); with whether their part-time status is regarded as temporary or whether they have a formal designation as part-time or temporary workers; and with whether they have negotiated their part-time status from a permanent full-time position or have become contract lawyers hired through an agency that handles temporary employment.[39] (This study was almost entirely limited to part-time lawyers who are not temporary contract lawyers.) The attitudes of coworkers and supervisors also help to create an environment in which part-time lawyers find themselves either valued or belittled.

Mechanisms That Stigmatize Part-Time Status

While a number of lawyers who work part-time schedules find it to be a positive personal experience at work and at home, a substantial number find they must confront reactions that range from nonspecific and unarticulated resentment and anger to almost hostile behavior.

Verbal and nonverbal communication: Because part-time positions are officially legitimate in any work environment in which they have developed, it is rare for coworkers or supervisors to openly state their opposition to them. Disapproval is communicated nonetheless through snide comments, sarcasm, slights, and nonverbal behavior.

It was good fortune, according to Stephanie Laughton, when a merger between her old firm and a new firm created the opportunity to negotiate a part-time partnership. Still, as she settled into her new job and tried to manage the stress of stretching her part-time schedule to cover a full-time workload, she found herself the target of colleagues' comments such as "Where are you when we need you?" Two years later, Laughton returned to a full-time schedule because she couldn't any longer face the stigma of part-time status.

An older associate in a midsize firm who entered law school and began a second career in her late 30s, Donna Carter, said she knew exactly why colleagues forget which days she works. "It's just a little whack, getting the dig in," she said. This carried a particular sting because Carter worked part-time out of necessity; one of her children had a grave illness. Similarly, Nancy Drager, a part-time litigator at a small firm, reported a continual trickle of snide remarks.

Sometimes lawyers who have worked part-time fail to support their part-time colleagues. Laurel Anderson, a corporate finance lawyer at a large firm, took offense when a former part-time attorney who returned to a full-time schedule made obnoxious comments about part-time people.

Others said they heard "playful" wisecracks from colleagues when they first started part-time work. Charlotte Wise, one of two attorneys in a large corporation who were granted part-time schedules, has heard her share of these wisecracks. Though Wise feels many were meant to belittle her, she also thinks they revealed a bit of envy among colleagues and clients:

> "Gee, I'd love to have a day off...ha ha ha." I'd say, "Look, they're not '*off.*' If you knew what I did on my days 'off,' I think you'd rather be at work."

Clarissa Hoskins reported she was the target of "slighting by forgetting" in the legal department of the large corporation where she works:

> They use...[voice-mail messages] to joke: "It's Wednesday—are you here?" or, "It's Thursday—are you home?"...I think to some extent they are really jealous that I don't have the grind every single day. I think in some ways they are being kind of ribbing in a nice and friendly way. I think it is just a topic of conversation like, "Oh, hi, are you here today?" But it annoys us—it really annoys us.

Clients' objection to part-time work: Clients' reactions to working with a part-time lawyer run a range from cooperative to feeling inadequately served. Ruth Tucker, a specialist in real estate law, made the request to go part-time at a large firm three years ago so she could spend part of her time doing volunteer tenant/landlord work at a legal services agency. Her colleagues supported her, but a major client complained "six times over the course of this year that he lost a lawyer by getting her because she wasn't there the entire time."

As an ultimate sign of rejection, clients stigmatize part-time lawyers by avoiding or refusing to work with them. Some attorneys reported that clients wanted to know why they have to work with someone who "could be gone tomorrow," falsely equating reduced hours with a lack of long-term job commitment. Yet we found that the part-time lawyers we interviewed rarely leave jobs they enjoy unless they are laid off.

Symbolic treatment that highlights differential status: In addition to slights and digs, a few part-time attorneys reported dismissive treatment in law offices that highlighted their second-class citizenship in other ways. These included not being given offices, business cards, or other tangible indicators of professional status.

A lawyer at a large insurance company, Jean Graber, described the status consciousness of the culture and how it undermined her rank within the organization. She was made to feel like a second-class citizen by not being given a name plate on her office door. She also was not permitted to have business cards or letterhead with her name on them. Further indignities included not being invited to the departmental retreat and exclusion from the company's organizational chart.

Examples of second-class treatment were offered by Katherine Marx, a civil litigator in a small firm before she was laid off. The full-time partners rented her office on the days she was not at work, highlighting her contingent status, and as a further insult, held the firm's cocktail hour on the days she was not in the office. Miriam Greer was assigned work space in a paralegal's office by the managing partner in her firm. She mounted a successful campaign to get a lawyer's office, well aware of the symbolic message the assignment carried:

> [The lawyer who brought me in] said "Don't worry,... [a lawyer's office] was promised to you."... He fought for me. But if I hadn't gotten involved... I might have gotten stuck in a paralegal's office.

Second-class status was reinforced by pension inequities for part-time work, according to part-timers and their colleagues in a government agency we studied. There, pensions accrued not according to the calendar but according to the proportion of a year worked. A lawyer working on a half-time schedule had to work 20 years for her pension to vest rather than the 10 years required of full-time lawyers. Attorneys regard this rule as punitive rather than economically based. Ellen Russell, a part-time attorney in the office, explained:

> The way the [pension] law is written it's supposed to include part-time lawyers who are permanent.... We weren't temporary folks who came on for six months and... [were expected] to disappear.... The pension really ought to vest in the same 10 years, because it's 10 years of real time.

As we will see in the chapter on mobility, stigma also was implicit in the ways in which time was calculated for seniority and advancement of part-time lawyers. Arthur Kant, the attorney who earlier was quoted as anticipating stigmatization, had a telecommuting arrangement in a government agency. Although he found support as "a test case" in his agency, he was concerned that he would have to hide his work arrangement when applying for a better job elsewhere because of the sentiment that work performed outside the office didn't count as "real work."

Collateral Damage: The "Halo Effect" of Part-Time Stigmatization

Holding a stigmatized status may prompt others to unfairly attribute failures to the person in question. For example, the lawyer in the job-sharing situation described earlier told us that when work is not completed efficiently it's blamed on the job-sharing arrangement, whereas if one works full time, failure is blamed on a heavy workload:

> If you're in a job share, they'll blame it on the fact you're not there every day—that you're not getting your work done. Instead of if you're full-time, you're just overburdened because you're busy.

Gender and Stigma

Stigma attached to part-time work cannot be separated from attitudes and general norms toward gender roles in the larger society.

As the sociologist Arlie Hochschild (1979) has noted, these extend to the "emotion norms" that attach to the nurturing aspect of the mother's role, which involves not only feeding and educating children, for example, but deeply felt mother love. Although elsewhere in this book we argue for the legitimacy of motherhood as a justification for part-time schedules, it is important to point out that men may be stigmatized if they request or engage in part-time work in order to spend more time with their children (Goffman, 1963).

The reasons one gives for requesting a part-time schedule are taken into account by those who grant the option in many circumstances. In the past, it would have been unimaginable for men to request a part-time schedule to take care of children (unless they had been widowed). Firms accepted as legitimate, however, men's requests for time off to participate in public domain activities, such as a political campaign or business venture. In rare cases, an attorney might take a sabbatical to write a book, or an extended leave to hold elective political office.

In these cases, the reduced schedule (in terms of yearly output) was not called "part-time," and was regarded as temporary. Thus, the less-than-full-time schedules that men have had recourse to have not been called "part-time." Labeling, according to the sociologist Howard Becker (1963), places the actor in circumstances where it is hard to continue the routines of everyday life. Thus, part-time professionals develop repertoires for avoiding the label that stigmatizes them if they can.

Stigmatizing the Performance of Multiple Roles

Antipathy to women's assumption of multiple roles contributes to the stigmatization of part-time work. Some writers attribute the hostility reported by a number of part-time lawyers to a backlash against women's progress in high-level occupations (Epstein, 1987; Faludi, 1991).

Lawyers reported comments expressing disapproval of their attempts to play roles historically regarded as incompatible: those of attorney and mother. Some reported that colleagues and acquaintances seemed to think that anyone performing these roles part time showed a lack of commitment to both roles. Thus we find an underlying disapproval for attempts to perform multiple roles.

For example, when Melissa Fiske asked for a reduced schedule in the large financial institution for which she worked, her supervisor commented: "If you want to be a lawyer, be a lawyer. If you want to be a mother, be a mother." Ellen Barnes, who worked for more than 10 years in a government legal office, said:

> It's a very tricky thing to work part-time....You're really neither fish nor fowl.... For full-time committed attorneys, you've copped out or...fallen off the track, or you've made much too big a compromise,... [they] can't take you *that* seriously. And conversely, you have the same sort of stuff from stay-at-home mothers who, of course, view *their* role as very important.... It is,...but they think you're some other creature because...part of the day you're someplace else.

A double stigma was experienced by George Marks, the part-time lawyer-husband of a part-time attorney. He suffers an even greater onus than his wife, because he violates both time and manhood norms by attempting to combine his professional role with an active role as an involved father. As his wife reported, feedback from colleagues and friends communicated their view that "real men do not work at home."

Techniques for Reducing the Stigma of Part-Time Status

Erving Goffman (1963) wrote in his book *Stigma* that some people try to anticipate and evade the negative consequence of a stigmatized status. One way is "passing"—that is, acting as if one were "normal"[40]—in this case, as if one were a full-time professional; another is information control.

Passing: The ability to pass by making the stigmatized status invisible reflects the relational aspect of stigmatization. One can bluff opposing litigators by seeming to work full-time or by keeping clients unaware of one's schedule so that opponents and clients feel they are interacting with and relying on a full-time professional. In these cases, the relationship with the part-time lawyer is based on the client's perception that she or he is diligently at work and available at all times.

Information control: Passing rests partly on the ability and opportunity to manage information about oneself (Goffman, 1963: 91). As we shall describe later, technology is helpful for this, and so is the use of gatekeepers such as secretaries. Part-time lawyers consider these factors all the time in making decisions about whether to reveal their status or hide it.

A part-time associate pointed out that unless she has ongoing work with clients or co-counsel, she is not inclined to reveal she works part time. She feels it is important to acknowledge the fact to continuing clients, not only for scheduling purposes but also as a way to explain why she does not have a supervisory title.

Sandra Karp felt no need to hide or play down her part-time arrangement. Her boss, a woman Karp described as extremely supportive, worked well with her. But she took the advice of a colleague working in her department on a contract basis that she shouldn't let her arrangement be widely known and should maintain a low profile. Thus, while others talked about the career advantages of high visibility, she noted wryly that she "was striving for invisibility." The same kind of invisibility was sought by Deborah Finkelstein, a lawyer who had left a large firm that had several part-timers, but, she said, "You couldn't tell who they were; or they wouldn't tell you what their deal was. These were always secret things."

The passing strategy, called "covering" by Goffman (1963: 102), was cultivated by Deborah Pinkerton, a part-time associate. Pinkerton found ways to remain physically invisible even when she was working in her office, keeping the door closed and ordering lunch to be sent in, so that she would not be missed when not in the office. She hoped to give the impression that she was always there even if unseen.

John Logan, a supervisor in the legal department of a government agency who has worked part time in the past, told us that he had felt he had to hide his part-time status from adversaries. As he reported: "Litigation is a game of bluff, and you want your adversaries to think you're working hard all the time against them." Karen Scott, a recently laid-off part-time government staff attorney, told of her subterfuge:

> Part-timers also have to accommodate court schedules, but it was an unwritten rule that *we* developed, we never *ever* advised the court that we were working less than 100 percent.... We would never say that we were unavailable because we had a part-time schedule.... We decided that it was [a bad idea] to be asking for more time [to accommodate our limited worktime schedule].... We didn't think that the court would buy it, we didn't think that it was any of their business.

And another part-time government attorney commented:

> I don't like to bring it up...because I think it connotes an unserious[ness] to an awful lot of people.... It's amazing how most people don't notice.... It's not like they expect a phone call to be returned within three hours. If it's returned the next day, that's perfectly legitimate.

Orders from her firm to pass as a full-time attorney were reported by Serena Woodward, a part-time associate in a major firm. Her secretary transferred calls to her home on her day off. Other respondents reported that some lawyers gave their home phone numbers to clients without telling them it was a home number.

The lack of face-to-face interaction (or "face time") was not a problem to clients, according to one lawyer:

> [My part-time schedule] wasn't really advertised, because lots of the people that I dealt with were not in the same location. They would just call. And I would either be there or not. And I would always call back within a day or two. And I found that most people…weren't confronting me as full-time or part-time; all they cared about was, "Was my work done?" And "Were my calls returned within a reasonable amount of time?" And since I always returned my phone calls—which was something that a lot of other people didn't do—that [gained me] a lot of goodwill. People didn't care.

A part-time in-house counsel who rose to become a vice president of her corporation did not tell clients she was part-time because "it didn't come up."

"Passing" was a game for some attorneys, but a number of them played the game out of shame they felt from perceived negative evaluations. As the sociologist Thomas Scheff (1988) has described, even in the absence of obvious sanctions, the part-time lawyer may anticipate rejection (criticism, passive-aggressive jokes, withdrawal by colleagues)—and consequently may behave in ways that minimize the visibility of his or her deviance. A continual process of self-monitoring—in which one takes cues from the situation and from the self-imagined disgrace—serves as a mechanism of social control.

Although part-time work is often stigmatized, its definition as a deviant professional work style varies depending on the institution, attitudes of coworkers and supervisors, and the acceptance or rejection of the lawyer who has chosen to work that way. The stigmatizing process is compounded because most part-time lawyers are women, who still are confronting the consequences of stereotypes that question their professional roles.

We have seen that lawyers are sensitive to the ways in which part-time status is deprecated by unnecessary and unwarranted behavior by colleagues whose intent, conscious or not, is to undermine its legitimacy.

In the next chapter we identify the structural, cultural, and psychological factors that act to make part-time work possible without social stigma.

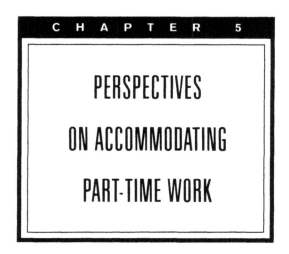

CHAPTER 5

PERSPECTIVES ON ACCOMMODATING PART-TIME WORK

Receptivity to Part-Time Work

In some institutional settings part-time work is not stigmatized. In them, gate-keepers may perceive it as offering benefits to the organization, or they may regard it as a legitimate alternative to full-time work. Economic benefits may be calculated based on the investment in workers that might otherwise be lost, continued access to the technical skills of attorneys who otherwise might leave, or because personal relations have evolved and, with it, a desire to ensure goodwill.

Some of the lawyers studied have had positive experiences with part-time work in their organizations. They were interviewed about the factors that contribute to acceptance of part-time work.

Benefits to the Organization

Attracting and retaining the services of talented attorneys: The law firm Skadden, Arps, Slate, Meagher and Flom used part-time attorneys during a period of rapid growth to the benefit of both the firm and the lawyers who wished to work reduced schedules. Skadden became well known when it took on more than 40 part-time lawyers during the economic boom of the 1980s (Caplan, 1993). The firm attracted the services of talented women during this time. Although many part-time attorneys found themselves to be the first to go in the economic downturn of the profession in the early 1990s, the rise in Skadden's fortunes in the latter part of the decade again made the firm receptive to part-timers. Cynthia Fuchs Epstein, an author of this book, heard of these developments from a New York City attorney while both were attending a Stanford University law conference. The lawyer, a founding member of the part-time lawyers network attached to the Association of the Bar of the City of New York, had herself found an "ideal" reduced schedule position at a large law firm that suited her well. In 1997 her talents were in demand, and her desire to work part time was regarded as a benefit, as it had been at Skadden in the early 1980s. Part time was no longer thought of as merely a concession to the requests of lawyers pressing for schedules to accommodate their personal needs. Rather, the arrangement satisfied lawyers' needs and those of the organization.

In corporate settings too, part-time arrangements allow firms to obtain the services of talented attorneys who otherwise might not work for them. Kenneth McGreevy, general counsel at a major accounting firm, saw part-time options as pragmatic. His view was that if you can make your employees happy, you can attract a higher caliber applicant and get better work. It was not, therefore, an accommodation or an exception when he offered support and advice to his legal team about how to work out a job-sharing situation. As a general counsel, he offered part-time work as a way to compete for the services of an attorney who had been offered a high-salary full-time job by a major accounting firm. As he recounted it:

> When I approached her to hire her, I told her that I could not give her the same salary that she was getting at X and Y [a major accounting firm] on a full-time basis, but what I was willing to do was accommodate her desire for a four-day workweek.

McGreevy reported that if a corporation is going to compete to get talented lawyers, it must support alternative work arrangements. His statement clearly laid out a rationale that most part-timers wish were common:

> Those old traditional work norms that you come here and you're prepared to stay at your desk until the job is done, however many days a week, however many months a year, sacrificing vacation pay...because you're a man and you don't have to go home and take care of children.... That isn't the world anymore.... Maybe it never was the world. But it certainly isn't the world anymore.... I've always thought that with increasing percentages of professionals being female that the big firms, all the firms, every firm, is going to have to figure out how to change the working norms to accommodate them.

He added that other developments make part-time work a feasible alternative:

> It's also technology and the ways that work is being done. People are spending more time out of the office, whether they're working at home or whether they're spending time on the client's premises. The old paradigm is changing also. People are spending time on the road. They're showing up at clients' premises with their laptop computer, and they're staying there for two, three, or four days at a time. And they come into the office once a week. Or not at all. Sometimes people are experimenting with flexible offices. You don't have a fixed office. They assign you whatever office or cubicle is available for that day. Then you plug your laptop into the office network, and all of your e-mail gets directed there automatically.

Jeffrey Riggs, another supervisor, also described the benefits of working with part-time lawyers:

> I started working with [Sara] and would ask what her schedule was for the week and delegate projects that I felt were self-contained and that she could do within the time period that was allotted. It was useful to me, it was easy for her to get done—she was very responsible—and she did a good job. So it was to my benefit to have it work for her.

•   •   •

> I also employ a part-time man.... If I have a big project he works on it, and then when I don't need him he goes off and [does his other business].... It works out very well.

•   •   •

> Similarly, a woman [came] back to work...three days a week. I got a tremendous amount out of it.... I got brains. I got hard work. So I didn't have somebody there the minute I had to, but most of the time it was only in someone's mind that [a task] had to be done that minute.

Neila Rohrer, a part-time staff attorney, raved about support from her immediate superior, who was amenable to part-time work from the start; she said he told her, "'I'd rather have you four days than no days'—which is exactly what I wanted to hear."

Corporations may also take steps to make clear that part-time is valued. For example, Stephanie Neilson, a part-time in-house staff attorney, was impressed by the fact that her company recruited a temporary replacement for her during her second maternity leave. This made her feel that her place was protected and she was appreciated:

I was really thrilled because I thought that gave my position real weight. [The corporation] held a spot for me and...created...the sense, that "Yes, it's important enough to hire somebody to do that work."

Personal relations: With one exception, none of the lawyers interviewed for this study began his or her career by working part-time. Rather, they negotiated part-time arrangements after proving professional worth to an organization and, in many instances, after developing strong social ties with more senior supervisors—partners in law firms or supervising attorneys in corporations and government. Lawyers typically requested part-time work only after a long-term professional relationship had been established.

Rita Swenson, a part-time associate with a large firm's product liability practice, spoke fondly of a senior partner who respected the boundaries of her part-time schedule:

Jonathan [the partner] actually apologizes for calling me at home, which I tell him he can do at any time. He says, "I'm sorry if I'm bothering you at home," but he really doesn't do it that much. He is a person who has children, and I think he is sensitive to...[the fact that] when I'm home, I can't do work—I don't have live-in help. He knows if I say, "I can't come in," I can't come in. He hears [children] crying in the background so he knows I can't.

A partner whose own schedule restrictions, for religious reasons, were accommodated was seen to be more sensitive than many other colleagues to the needs of Marina Foster, a part-time associate in a large firm's tax practice:

There are certain days when he doesn't work. I think this is something that might make him more sensitive—because he's an orthodox Jew, and he doesn't work Friday nights or Saturdays. And I think that he came through this firm having to tell people, "I can't work Friday night." So when he sees that I can't work on a day, he's sensitive to that.

Indicators of Receptivity

A number of part-time attorneys reported they did not feel that they were treated differently than full-time attorneys. Some reported being invited to all staff meetings and receiving routine communications. Moreover, the ease with which attorneys move back and forth between part-time and full-time work is an indicator of the positive attitude of a legal workplace. Eric Golden, a corporation counsel who has been with the same litigation division for eight years, reported he does not know which of his 25 or so attorney colleagues are part-time—a sign, he thinks, that there is no fixed-tiered system. Further, the fluidity of movement between full-time and part-time status is facilitated by a work organization in which most lawyers work autonomously on cases.

Andrea Geller, a part-time associate in a large law firm, does not believe her commitment is questioned by clients:

> I don't think that they think they're getting somewhat less of a commitment or something like that. If I say to them "We need to speak tomorrow," or they get me on a conference call they know they're calling me at home, and I do whatever needs to be done.

Strategies and Attitudes of Supervisors

Supervisors' attitudes can frame a receptivity to part-time work and define it as legitimate. A full-time general counsel we interviewed, for example, was not only receptive to part-time work but protective of it. He ensured that part-time lawyers were not overwhelmed with work or required to stay extra hours (except for emergencies) by having a weekly luncheon meeting with staff and offering his advice to part-time lawyers. As he explained:

> I tried to keep close track of it. And watching the time sheet was one [way] of doing it, but also I tried to talk to [the part-time attorneys] regularly, and keep up with how things [were] going. That's one of the reasons I started the legal department lunch thing...a formal time set aside each week where we had to say to each other what we're doing. Kick ideas around with each other...like "Oh, yeah, I did something like that." Or, "You ought to look at the so-and-so file." ...Or, "We've done that already."

Sometimes a particular supervisor may become committed to a part-time program even when the company culture is resistant to it. In this situation, part-time policies may be implemented without becoming institutionalized. A number of attorneys came to realize how extensively they had been relying on their immediate supervisors to champion their cause, especially when those supervisors were no longer there. Felice Lamont voiced concern for many others when she recounted her own experience:

> After this part-time program was first established...(maybe we were deluding ourselves)...I didn't feel marginalized.... I felt that we were making very valuable contributions. But I do think over time, that maybe that was an illusion.... The company was not making a commitment to being supportive of mothers and families and alternative career schedules—it was just this one individual, my boss, who...was willing to support it and implement it.... This was just kind of a little blip.

The Impact of Law Specialties on Part-Time Work

One question that is often raised about the practicality of part-time work for lawyers is whether it can be accommodated in specific practices. This has been a particular concern in large law firms. There, the question is whether certain areas of specialization are better suited to this type of schedule. It may be easier to adopt such arrangements in specialties like trusts and estates, tax, and regulatory law, which are less likely to require rapid solutions to clients' problems and therefore allow most lawyers in them to work more predictable hours. For lawyers practicing in the areas of litigation and corporate transactions, however, the difficulties become more pronounced.

Yet most of the associates in our study of large law firms who had experience working part-time had done so in litigation or corporate specialities—relatively large departments at the law firms where interviews were conducted. It was paradoxical to find negative attitudes about the advisability of working part-time by these lawyers. Of course, they heard these views often expressed by their colleagues.

As far as litigators were concerned, the pressures of preparation for trial and courtroom appearances seem to make this area of legal practice particularly incompatible with part-time schedules. Robert Malcher, a litigator, framed the difficulties in this way:

> The thing that's always driven me crazy about litigation is that you can never make any plans, your hours are always uncertain down to the last minute.... You can't say, "It's Friday afternoon at five. I'll wait until Tuesday." You have to just do it.

Tess Oppenheim, a partner, drew similar conclusions:

> Litigation is tough. You have less control of the court deadlines, and things like that come up.... If you work only a certain few days a week there's no guarantee that there won't be a conference or an argument scheduled on one of the days you're theoretically off.

Yet Toni Morris, a part-time litigator, believed that greater flexibility was possible:

> Many times someone else can fill in for something I'm doing, if I don't happen to be around. That's not to say that if a judge has a hearing just on Fridays I won't show up, but litigators are often substituted for each other.

Lawyers in corporate practice thought their specialty was least compatible with part-time work, but said other specialties could accommodate it. George Fischer, the head of a corporate practice group, suggested:

> For litigation, it's easier than corporate. On a deal that involved a major SEC matter, I would not think about staffing it with a part-timer as a significant part of the team, just because I don't want to have to bring a substitute in.

Morris Altman, another corporate partner, thought similarly:

> It doesn't work in transaction work, where what you do is race against the clock. If you can't provide service you shouldn't hold yourself out to be in the service business.

Thus we see that the will to accommodate part-time work has a great deal to do with its success. There are, no doubt, situations in which it is difficult to manage work demands with lawyers on part-time schedules, but in each sphere of practice, avenues of opportunity exist if supervisors and colleagues are oriented to making an abbreviated workweek work.

CHAPTER 6

CALCULATING THE ECONOMICS OF PART-TIME WORK

Time is money in the workplace—especially the legal workplace. But the question of whether part-time work "pays" for both the organization and the person engaged in it is not as simple an economic calculation as it sounds. Although law firms and other organizations know that contract lawyers cost them less than regular employees do,[41] we know of no law firms that have worked out a cost accounting scheme for regular, on-staff part-time lawyers that compares their productivity to the investment in them—although some firms certainly attempt to evaluate productivity. Although the expectation is that there is a *quid pro quo* of effort to output and of compensation to contribution, concepts such as productivity are subjectively evaluated or impossible to calculate (like the reputation of attorneys and their ability to attract clients) (Hagan and Kay, 1995). Some executives believe that part-time professional work is profitable for an organization; others believe it is not. Which conclusion is reached often depends on how the equation is set up and calculated and which variables are used. General findings are positive. In a review of studies, Blank (1990) found that firms that use part-time workers tend to indicate that there is less absenteeism and less turnover among them than among full-time workers. Further, part-time workers take fewer breaks and less personal time while on the job. However, to date, at least, the economics of part-time work is partially socially constructed and partially a product of rational cost accounting. Furthermore, since part-time work is regarded as primarily a "woman's issue," the calculation of worth is not only tied to beliefs about productivity but to executives' views about how committed and productive women are in comparison with men[42] and to views about the nature of motherhood. Finally, the economics of part-time work has a symbolic function. That is, the ways in which an organization thinks about and approaches the negotiation of compensation, overhead, productivity, benefits, bonuses, and promotion constitutes its "mentality" about such issues and conveys a message to the staff at all levels about its attitudes toward part-time work.

From the organizational point of view, the question arises of whether a lawyer returns more than she or he costs in terms of investment, overhead, and compensation. The calculation has different meanings in the different spheres of law.

Within law firms, compensation and associated costs can be compared and linked to revenues in terms of billable hours of part-time and full-time lawyers. Although diary and time sheets were used to keep track of time in some firms in the 1950s, it was not until the 1960s that billing for lawyers hours became the standard method of calculating the fees charged clients (Hagan and Kay, 1995) as an "objective" measure of the work done for them. Although partners in firms and managers in corporate legal departments can calculate the overhead costs of an office, support staff, outlay of benefits, and the highly nebulous factor of impact on the effectiveness and morale of other employees, such costs are rarely figured directly against the productivity of lawyers.

Scholars of the economic culture of large firms (Galanter and Palay, 1991; Gilson and Mnookin, 1985) have emphasized that there is a turn toward monitoring productivity in law firms by tracking billable hours. Because of the persistent view that lawyers who work fewer hours than the high standards set in large firms (upward of 2,000 billable hours a year) are less worthy, hours worked and billed become a measure of productivity (in human capital terms), with low producers regarded as "free riders" (Hagan and Kay, 1995; Leibowitz and Tollinson, 1980). Part-time workers, however, and many of the partners who negotiate part-time assignments with them, do calculate productivity *within* each hour worked. However it is calculated, firms expect to make a considerable profit on the work of associates (Galanter and Palay, 1991).

Associates in large law firms in New York all started full-time work as new law graduates at salaries of $83,000 a few years ago (the figure today is closer to $90,000 for starting salaries), and by the time they are senior associates who might ask for part-time schedules they probably earn between $125,000 and $175,000 a year in salaries and bonuses. These lawyers' work is billed to clients by the firm at $200 to $350 an hour. A private study of 555 large firms across the country completed in 1994 found that fifth-year associates, who tend to be in their late 20s, made an average of $75,830 per year (Hacker, 1997: 132). Even on part-time schedules they make substantial salaries at rates of between three-fifths and four-fifths of these amounts.[43]

For partners, individual shares of law firm profits range from $200,000 to more than $1 million depending on the firm. The New York firm of Wachtell, Lipton, Rosen, and Katz, on the high end of the spectrum, netted its partners an average compensation of $1.6 million in 1995 (Hacker, 1997), for example. Part-time incomes can be considerable for associates and very high for the very tiny number of part-time partners.

Although there are no agreed standards for law firm cost accounting, firms are concerned with assessing their lawyers' economic value (Gilson and Mnookin, 1985). This issue always comes up in the review process. But law firms sell a service whose quality cannot be judged prior to purchase. The outcome of many legal transactions is indeterminate when begun. The verdict of a trial or the efficacy of legal advice is unknowable before a client hires an attorney. At the same time, the results of many legal services may be crucial to a corporation's or an individual's well-being. As a result, when clients purchase legal services they have no measure other than a lawyer's or a firm's reputation as a predictor of quality. Firms, for their part, are repositories of "reputational" capital that rely on the human capital and social networks of their partners and associates.

The ability to retain talented attorneys is crucial to maintaining or enhancing the reputation of a firm. The skill and social networks of a lawyer adhere to the person and are not divisible. This concept is clearly represented in the retention of senior "of counsel" attorneys. A part-time attorney's skills and networks are not in and of themselves proportional to the amount of time at work. Furthermore, it is accepted that all lawyers bring skills to an organization that are not reflected in billable hours. An innovative legal strategy, a lead on business possibilities, or management abilities may not translate into any individual's increased billable hours.

In the legal departments of government agencies and corporations, where the practice of law is not usually meant to generate revenue, matters are also complicated, but of course, lawyers here make considerably lower salaries.[44]

In-house legal departments handle the routine legal work of the corporation and usually contract with large firms for their complicated and high-profile work. Corporations increasingly handle work in-house in order to reduce expenses. Often, in-house legal matters are geared to routine actions and research to save the company money (*e.g.,* filing motions to ward off lawsuits and handling employee benefits disputes). Although they typically are less pressured, many in-house attorneys are asked to work long hours from time to time. In some larger corporations, legal departments use a billable-hours accounting system, but such calculations are used only to assess attorney and department productivity, not to generate revenues. In some cases, however, general counsels use billable-hours data to bargain for larger legal department budgets. Government legal departments carry out the political will of the state through the courts and other juridical bodies; they are not income-generating although they must be cost-effective.

In all three cases, minimizing costs of the legal department (or firm) is desirable but not necessarily crucial. A law firm can justify increased spending by increased revenues.

On the other hand, in both corporations and government, budget allocations are the result of political decisions. Executives and managers from both sectors are almost unanimous in agreeing that part-time policies allow them to hire and retain exceptional talent—ironically, the very lawyers whose value is diminished in law firms because they do not wish to work full-time. Some believe any additional costs of hiring part-time people are worth paying because of the excellence of the product per hour worked by such lawyers.

So what seems to be a relatively simple accounting calculation is actually quite complex. Trade-offs enter into determining the value and cost to organizations of part-time work. On the one hand, increased costs may incur from covering the overhead of an office, support staff, and benefits. Added management difficulties and unpredictability of the ready responsiveness of part-time lawyers may also have a price. But part-timers offer benefits of seniority and expertise that would be more costly if offered by a full-time person.

The influx of women into the legal community poses problems of accounting that interact with gender. The stress of balancing their work and family commitments leads women to reduce work hours, with the expectation that they will have a lower pay scale and a poor career ladder (Rhode, 1997). They are not usually in a good position to bargain, although most of the women we interviewed seemed to be conscious of their worth. Bringing this evaluation in line with those of the decision-makers is not always easy. This is because the sense of gain or loss from making part-time work possible is variously interpreted. On the most positive side is the comment of Paul Neurath, a senior partner in a large midtown firm:

> I've been increasingly persuaded that we've been kidding ourselves to hire and train all these women and then lose them. As an economic proposition that's an absurdity.

On the negative side, Charles Smythe, senior partner in a large downtown firm, insisted: "You cannot run a practice on a bunch of part-timers. It doesn't work."

A part-timer may question whether the pay is fair for the time and effort and the efficiency of output, whether or not measured by actual time—for example, the speed and efficiency of work time without downtime at lunch or socializing on the job.

Many employers attempt to match the percentage of time spent at work with pay (*e.g.*, four days work equal four-fifths pay). This works well in sectors with generally standard hours of employment (such as a 9-to-5 day for the government), but it is difficult to calculate when the workday may range from eight to 18 hours. In firms where lawyers may often be expected to work seven days a week, but which conceptualize a four-day schedule as four-fifths of a workload, four-fifths pay may seem unfair to full-time employees.

On the other hand, many part-time lawyers who have agreed to a reduced workload and are paid accordingly find that they work the same number of hours as full-time colleagues. Although this is unusual (because a good proportion of part-time lawyers insist on restricting their hours of work), it does happen during times when there are pressing business needs for overtime work or when the workload for other full-time lawyers is reduced because client demand has diminished.

There are symbolic considerations in the calculation of productivity and the accompanying views about how they should be rewarded. For example, a common pattern is illustrated by Rebecca Alford, an associate in her late 30s who works 80 percent of the standard minimum billable hours in the corporate department of a large firm and receives 80 percent of a full-time associate's salary. Unlike her full-time colleagues, however, she cannot count as hours worked time spent at seminars, bar association committee meetings, or department lunches. Another pattern, widespread in government legal offices, makes part-time attorneys ineligible for merit awards. (Attorneys who exceed expectations are given cash bonuses for good work, a criterion that many part-time attorneys wholeheartedly believe they fulfill, notwithstanding their reduced hours.) Some law firms and corporation legal departments reduce salaries for part-time lawyers by about 5 percent, in one attorney's words, "to make up for the unused portion of overhead."

Cost-saving measures like these, some of them trivial, likely serve a function other than economic. According to the social psychologist Yiannis Gabriel, these behaviors are insults[45] that help "to establish a pecking order among members of a collectivity and as such, are part of a trading process not merely instruments for establishing inclusion and exclusion, domination and subordination, but also finer gradations of status and power."

Thus, each decision to withhold a reward or perquisite that full-time attorneys enjoy, however unimportant, has the symbolic function of establishing and reinforcing a status hierarchy in which part-time attorneys are regarded as lower in rank.

As we see, the economic assessment of part-time work is highly variable and is relative to the perceptions and pressures experienced in individual workplaces and of the openness or resistance of particular supervisors to alternative work arrangements.

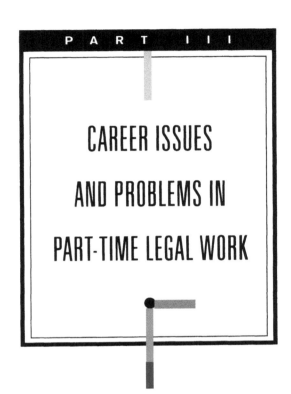

PART III

CAREER ISSUES
AND PROBLEMS IN
PART-TIME LEGAL WORK

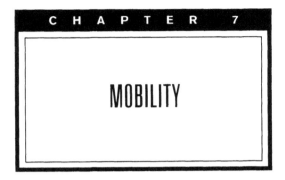

MOBILITY

Progress in one's career is an American ideal, but it is not typical for all people, nor is it common in many occupations. For individuals, the concept of movement up a career ladder is linked with their community, ethnic background, and neighborhood (Willis, 1977). Furthermore, career progression is a fairly modern phenomenon, according to Modell and his colleagues (1978).[46] Because it is a contemporary ideal and because career progression in law is linked to professionalization, not moving ahead puts one at risk of being labeled deviant (Levin and Levin, 1991: 662). Of course, not all, or even most, young lawyers succeed in climbing the ladder and obtaining the brass ring of partnership, as it is called in large corporate law firms (Epstein *et al.,* 1995; Galanter and Palay, 1991; Smigel, 1964; Wilkins and Gulati, 1996), but they are supposed to try to move upward, especially in the areas of law where the pattern of mobility is most clearly defined.

Mobility is a good indicator of the regard with which lawyers are held and of their integration within the profession. Because even full-time, "on-track" attorneys depend on being identified as partnership material, based on subjective and objective criteria such as how hardworking they are (partially based on billable hours), their commitment, excellence, and their potential for client development, part-time attorneys are in a problematic situation.[47] The limited hours they work identify them as time deviants and define them as less committed and less hardworking than full-time attorneys. About 60 percent of a nationally representative sample of attorneys surveyed by the American Bar Association believed that reduced-hour or part-time employment limited opportunities for advancement including partnership (American Bar Association, 1991: 27); in a survey of large firms, 96 percent of associates (and 89 percent of partners) felt that willingness to work long hours was a factor considered important for promotion to partner (Landers, Rebitzer, and Taylor, 1996). That firms insist on unflagging availability and dedication to one's professional life as conditions for becoming a partner is well known. Sophia Merlin, an associate in a large firm, stated it frankly:

> If there are two people who are up for the same job, or are up for partnership and they are both equally qualified, somebody who is going to give more time is going to get it—and probably rightfully so.

Typically, we have seen that part-time lawyers are marginalized and are placed off the track toward professional advancement.[48]

Thus it is not surprising to find few part-time lawyers in positions of authority and prestige.[49] In our prior study of eight large corporate law firms (Epstein *et al.*, 1995), only three part-time partners were identified, and in the course of this study an interested partner in another large firm referred us to three partners in her firm who worked less than full time (one had already been a partner for many years before going part-time). The first woman to become president of the prestigious Association of the Bar of the City of New York, Barbara Paul Robinson, was also a trailblazer in becoming a partner in her firm, Debevoise & Plimpton, after working on a reduced schedule for four years after her second son was born. She became a partner in 1976 after returning to full-time work. This was two to three years later than she would have been made partner had she worked full time for all her 10 years at Debevoise (Klein, 1996), she told a reporter for the *National Law Journal*. Nina Levitt, a litigation partner in a high-profile corporate firm, also had a history of working a reduced schedule. She negotiated a four-day workweek, but when she was in the midst of litigation she worked up to 80 hours a week. The difference between her and the firm's full-time associates was that she could take some days off when work was not pressing. However, after working nine years in this part-time position she returned to full-time work and became a partner after an additional eight years. While Robinson's and Levitt's stories are unique, a growing number, though they are still only a handful (just 1.3 percent), of lawyers on reduced schedules have become partners.[50]

Some lawyers have advanced to non-equity partnerships, although there are no available figures. Some have risen to higher positions—although below that of partner, such as special counsel—in other legal workplaces. A title, however, such as "permanent associate," which was not uncommon before the 1960s "was viewed as a model of failure" (Galanter and Palay, 1992). Movement from part-time positions, while unusual, is beginning to be recognized as a possible track. For example, Debevoise & Plimpton now has a parental leave policy and a part-time program that does not affect the formal partnership track (Klein, 1996).

Studying part-time lawyers in government agencies, we found only four part-time supervisors, and one part-time supervisor was located in an in-house corporation setting.

This indicated a limited opportunity structure for part-time attorneys, who typically are held in lower ranks while full-time colleagues move up as they become senior. A few partners had been part-time at some point in their careers, but typically they had to compensate by working full-time longer than other individuals in their class. Some current part-time partners work 80 to 90 percent of what is considered a full-time load and easily match the number of billable hours carried by lawyers who are regarded as full-time in other settings.

A number of factors retard mobility, but others create opportunity for advancement. Part-time status also evokes attitudes from colleagues and clients that clearly have ramifications for advancement, as we saw in the chapter on stigmatization. And lawyers' commitments and ideology about their family obligations have an impact on their attitudes toward mobility.

Opportunity Structure

Economic and structural contexts: Advancement possibilities for part-time attorneys must be assessed within the economic climate affecting all lawyers, no matter which sector they are working in. The economic downturn of the late 1980s and early 1990s was singled out as a factor by a number of lawyers in the study because it led to a contraction in the job market that affected their prospects for job tenure or promotion. Firms that had rapidly expanded to handle the profusion of mergers and acquisitions during the 1980s instituted layoffs and slowed the consideration of associates for promotion to partnership in the early 1990s (Galanter and Palay, 1991).

In-house departments in corporations were affected by the mergers and by downsizing, and both meant that many lawyers lost their jobs. Attorneys working in the government faced furloughs in some agencies; and shifts in political administrations made the lawyers who retained their jobs anxious.[51]

In the mid-1990s some firms hired part-time or contract attorneys to meet the demand created by the new upsurge in the economy.[52] These firms, having been hurt by the economic downturn, wanted temporary or part-time attorneys because they required fewer obligations and offered more flexibility.

Organizational structure: In the private and public sectors alike, the organizational hierarchy of legal workplaces has only a few levels, and movement upward is very significant.

Private firms, in particular, have long been marked by a system with only two ranks, associate and partner,[53] although several gradations have been added in the last few years. Associates receive higher salaries and bonuses as they become more senior, but the move to partnership is a quantum jump, bringing a share in the firm's profits, decision-making authority, and a promise of tenure. After seven to 10 years, associates who are not elevated to partner typically leave the firm unless very special arrangements are made to retain them. As in academia, movement is "up or out."

Today, only a few firms retain a lock-step compensation system (once a model for all firms [Smigel, 1964]) in which all partners share the firm's profits equally. Now, most use a point system in which individual partners' contributions to the firm are assessed, such as their rainmaking achievements and their number of billable hours. The practice is known as "eat what you kill" (Caplan, 1993: 181). We found that firms with a lock-step compensation system find it easier to determine "fair" compensation for part-time partners because the partnership share is a fixed amount.

Some firms now differentiate between equity and non-equity partners.[54] It is theoretically easier to "make partner" in a firm in which partnership does not require giving a non-equity partner an equal share of profits, than in one in which movement from associate to partnership means the attainment of full equality.

Lawyers working in corporation legal departments also are limited by the constraints of a flat hierarchy with a general counsel and deputy counsel at the top and most of the company's other lawyers sharing the same rank below. In corporations, the general counsel is typically a senior officer in the organization and has power and authority in the decision-making process.

Government agencies generally have more rungs in their organizational ladders: Between entry-level and executive positions are typically supervisory titles. Occasionally, this is the case in large corporations, where "team leaders" or senior counsels assume managerial roles.

It is in the context of the different hierarchical pyramids, reward structures, and the other social changes identified earlier that mobility is assessed.

Attitudes toward part-time supervisory jobs: The opportunity structure also depends on the cultures of organizations and the attitudes of senior management and colleagues about the feasibility of having part-time lawyers as supervisors (Merton, 1957). Tied to the issue of mobility is the question of whether the work of supervisors and partners can be accomplished by lawyers working part-time schedules.

While nearly everyone agrees that it is difficult if not impossible to juggle a part-time schedule and effectively manage executive or partnership responsibilities, we encountered six part-time lawyers who were partners in law firms, and four who had supervisory positions in government offices. A number of senior part-time associates supervised junior associates in law firms. But a high degree of ambivalence marked even those firms with part-time supervisors. Questions such as these are asked: Do they deserve the status? Can their commitment be trusted? Is promotion of part-timers fair to full-timers? Part-time lawyers themselves were not of one mind on the answers. When we asked them what they thought about the feasibility of part-time supervision they offered important insights into the obstacles they faced and the conditions under which this arrangement works.

Elvira Borden, a supervising attorney in the federal court system, reported that her four-day workweek arrangement was doing well. Proud of her assiduous efforts to pull together a legal unit that was in disarray when she began work there a few years earlier, Borden took it as a complement that the judges with whom she worked closely were willing to accommodate her wish to spend more time at home with her two young sons. Yet, like others in the study who worked part time in managerial positions, she underscored the trade-offs. One of her main concerns, and a source of guilt, was whether she was "giving enough TLC" to recently hired attorneys on her staff. On the other hand, she thought that because of her absence from the office one day a week, lawyers on her staff had become more autonomous and organized.

Another senior attorney, Marsha Simpson, stated her ambivalence to part-time work in a very descriptive manner:

> If I were a senior VP hiring a VP to handle a very important area, would I want a part-time person in that job when I could have a full-time person—a man who has a wife staying at home to take care of all the household things, and he could focus on work? I don't know.
>
> • • •
>
> Does a workaholic do a better job? Personally I don't think so because they kind of overworry, and I think working part-time gives you a perspective. You have five hours to do it and you do it, in the five hours. You get it done. Could you spend 20 hours on a $5 project? Absolutely. You write your notes, you rewrite your notes.... You know, any lawyer knows that the work expands...to fit the time allotted to it.

Years of experience and established relationships with clients made the difference, according to Amy Harris, a supervising attorney at a nationally known insurance company. Overseeing the work of 45 lawyers, paralegals, and support staff, Harris thought her credibility gave her flexibility. It really depends on the person, she said:

> You really need interpersonal skills. It's not easy to work part time and be successful. It's also, it's not a "gimme." I mean, there are people who have come into the law department and they are very good lawyers. And they say, "Well how come you can do that [work part time] and I can't?" Well, because I've been here for a long time.

People who wish to maintain family priorities probably cannot be partners, according to Kate Attewell, a part-time trusts and estates lawyer who wishes her options for advancement were more open. She had left a large downtown law firm for a smaller firm because she saw that to make partner one had to "marry" the firm. Even in the new firm, Attewell suspected that the demands of partnership would require sacrifices of her family time:

> If I did become a partner, the sense of priority would probably have to change a little. And I'll give you a good example.... I was scheduled to go to Miami on assignment and to leave Monday at 6 at night, and I found out last week that my son is in a show at camp that they've been working on all summer. And it's on at 5 on Monday night, and my husband... is just starting a new job, and he has a bunch of new business prospects set up for the next three weeks.... He can't leave work to be at the show at 5. So I went in to Robert [the supervising partner] and told him I don't want to miss the show. I want to take an earlier flight, and he said, "Fine. Go and do it." I'm not sure if I were a partner that I would be able to say that.

From the perspective of partners who have traveled the prescribed route and now make partnership decisions themselves, young lawyers who are critics of the tremendous workload and pressing time demands are not partnership material. This is how Bill Korn, partner in a large midtown firm whose name often appears in the legal press, stated the case:

> There is a certain amount of prestige that goes along with being a partner... people think they can have all the gravy and none of the grief.... At some point you really will have to make up your mind about what is it you want out of life. If you want to be a partner in a law firm, fine, be a partner in a law firm. But don't say, "I want to be a partner because I like the idea of being a partner, but I really don't want to do the work that's involved." It isn't fair to other people.

Formal and Informal Policies

Some firms and organizations have policies covering part-time work, including rules on the possibility or impossibility of advancement (as noted in

Appendix B). But, as noted above, most organizations do not. None specify how lawyers might get back on a partnership track—by returning to full-time work for a certain period of time, for example. This may be due to low demand; few part-timers have actually come back to full-time work with aspirations to advance. Yet it also could be viewed as an indication that in law firms and in corporations a stereotyped view persists that part-timers are usually mothers who will not want to restart their careers.

Explicit policies: In a few instances, the question of a part-time schedule's impact on career mobility was clear. Emily Goldberg, a litigator in a large firm, pregnant with her second child at the time she was interviewed, said she was "derailed" from partnership:

> The book says you will not make partner on a part-time basis. And the reality is that even if you make it full-time, you can't then switch to part-time. So it is not…a career path here to be a part-time person.

In the unique case of a legal department of a large accounting firm, policies regarding mobility not only came to be well defined but were also favorable to part-time work, according to Jill Nelson, an attorney who spoke of her general counsel with great affection:

> [He was] totally supportive of me being part-time and still becoming a partner. So that was good news because prior to him saying that to me explicitly, I didn't even think it was a possibility. I was just grateful for having my situation [approved]; to have the possibility to become a partner on top of that was…icing on the cake.

Government agencies tend to have explicit guidelines barring part-time attorneys from promotion to management positions. Indeed in one legal department, we were told by several attorneys that they had to give up supervisory positions when they went part time. Yet resuming full-time status put them back on a management track. Though their supervisory "lines" were not held open for them, these attorneys managed to reacquire the positions some years later when they were ready to come back full-time.

Implicit understandings: But there are implicit understandings even in organizations that lack explicit policy statements that part-time status takes an attorney off the track for promotion. Most part-time attorneys are not at all surprised by this—they assume that one must be full time to be conferred with the prestige and responsibility that come with managerial and executive positions. Further, the culture of the legal profession (as well as other professions) is imbued with the notion that being part-time and having power are incompatible concepts; hence few seriously question the career-limiting effect of part-time work. Indeed, as we discuss later, many believe that exclusion of part-timers from advancement is a justified and reasonable policy.

Sandra Kitso, an attorney at a large corporation, knew without being told that her part-time status would curb her advancement opportunities. Even though title changes were occasionally offered to attorneys as they assumed added responsibilities, Kitso believed this was mainly window dressing. Moreover, what little room existed for real mobility at her company—such as to become a senior officer of the company or general counsel—clearly was out of bounds for part-timers:

> There was never any explicit discussion…[but] nobody needed to tell me that it [being part time] would probably hurt me.

While most lawyers take it for granted that going part-time means going off the serious promotion track, discrepant views are most pronounced around the question of whether part-time status is a permanent disqualification for promotion. Key concerns such as how long one will be required to work full-time (after having been part-time) before being considered for promotion are ambiguous at most organizations. Even when assured that advancement options will reopen once a full-time schedule is resumed, attorneys are skeptical.

A number of part-time attorneys reported they had been dissuaded from having aspirations about advancement because they were certain they would be stigmatized for years to come, even after returning to full-time work.

Time in Part-Time Service

Two patterns emerged in the study regarding the time-in-rank and part-timers' hours equation. There is ambiguity about how to count part-timers' time in service toward promotion, as well as about how long an attorney must wait after resuming a full-time schedule before being considered for promotion, if that is possible. These ambiguities reflect the notion that the stigmatizing effects of part-time schedules may linger and hinder mobility chances even after someone has resumed full-time service.

The time assessment issue is a sticky one not only because no clear guidelines spell it out in most organizations, but also because it goes deep into questions of fairness. Should a year of part-time work be equal to a year of full-time work? Should a year for a three-fifths-time lawyer be counted as three-fifths of a year? These questions may become controversial if competition for promotion opportunities arises between full-time and part-time attorneys.

A few attorneys pointed out that if time in service were counted literally (if years of service were calculated the same way, without regard for whether one was full- or part-time), then part-timers would be progressing in seniority at the same rate as full-timers. Hence, a part-time attorney might resume full-time practice and compete for promotion with colleagues who had been working full time for the same number of years. Several attorneys believed this would cause resentment among full-timers, who feel more deserving of promotion.

Speaking ardently about her predicament, Eleanor Teplitsky, a 14th-year associate at a large law firm (a very rare situation), described being told in a review that if she returned to full-time work, she could be considered for partnership. She was dubious, however, believing that even though technically she had more seniority than other full-time associates, the odds were against her advancement. She was certain that associates junior to herself who were putting in huge numbers of hours at work would be favored.

Robin Tensing, a lawyer in a government agency, ruminated about the complications involved in trying to count a part-timer's time in service. As an attorney in an office with a flexible work policy, Tensing was able to move back and forth between full-time and part-time work over the past five years to care for her two children after their births. She understood how full-time colleagues might be resentful if part-time lawyers did not lose seniority when they returned to full-time work:

> How do you put someone back in a track where there's other people that have seen themselves moving up, think they're next in line and suddenly you come back full-time and get jumped ahead?... That could be very bad for morale of some people that have been full-time all the time.

Yet, in some law firms part-time work is literally obliterating questions of seniority. Barbara Delroy, a litigator on intellectual property matters, reported that in her large firm part-time status positioned her as "forever a third-year associate." As she observed:

> What obviously is clear is that the firm wants to make part-time status punitive enough so that people will not be interested in doing it for very long.

Delroy told us at the time of the interview that she was actively looking for another job.

Indirect Obstacles to Mobility

A number of factors associated with part-time work contribute indirectly to stalling career progress. These include decreased opportunities to work on high-profile matters, take the lead on cases, network with colleagues, develop mentorship connections, or engage in business development (rainmaking). Such problems also affect full-time lawyers who, for reasons of prejudice or tradition—as in the cases of women or members of minorities (Wilkins and Gulati, 1996)—are not regarded as partnership material (Epstein, [1981] 1993).

Constraints on part-time lawyers do not occur in a vacuum. They evolve out of the exigencies of part-time schedules as well as individual choices. While organizations may exclude part-time lawyers from professional opportunities as a practical matter or even in an attempt to dissuade others from choosing the option, the sheer fact of working reduced hours prevents part-timers from engaging in the kinds of grooming activities that are crucial for advancement. Without opportunities to learn and become visible, lawyers cannot demonstrate the very qualities for which they are judged in promotion decisions: legal skill, leadership capability, social and collegial compatibility, organizational commitment, and, in private firms, rainmaking.

Quality of assignments: Some part-time lawyers report their legal assignments are good, but most complain that their work assignments decrease in quality when they go on a part-time schedule. A high level of work assignment is usually maintained only for the very few who bring in clients and are assigned to work on their matters. In the case of one part-time partner, this was a billion-dollar deal. However, most part-timers cannot "make rain" at that level or sustain the demanding level of attention required, and decreasing quality of assignments is identified as the most convincing argument against choosing a part-time schedule.

This applies across the board to lawyers in private firms, government agencies, and corporations. In whatever way "good" cases are defined within an organization—and this varies by sector and legal specialty—these cases are given only parsimoniously to part-time lawyers. Such assignments include high-profile and complex legal matters that challenge and provide a context for learning and also offer opportunities for visibility.

In some firms the most interesting work goes to those who demonstrate their willingness to be available at all times. This often leaves part-timers with mundane research and writing assignments, which earn them little credit and exposure.

The following account offered by Mitch Goddard, known as a fair-minded division chief of a city government's legal department, illustrates the prevalent view of administrators that it is best to assign part-time lawyers to matters which are neither time sensitive nor interactive with clients.

> I guess there's only so much that a part-timer can assume [at work].... You tend to give them an issue that isn't the fastest moving...more research oriented than

transactional. They tend to do research and writing rather than meeting with people and negotiating terms…a certain kind of issue [that] limits exposure…to the more active, people-oriented part of the practice. We do a lot of research and writing, but we also do a lot of meetings and phone calls and sort of hands-on, handholding of clients and…there's going to be less of that, when you're part-time because you're not…always available.

Although she believes she could manage most types of work, Madeleine McCollum, a part-time staff attorney at a large financial services institution, is excluded from high-level work:

[There] are certain high-visibility projects that [the general counsel] feels he can't give to me because I am part time…. Things that he handles are on a faster track, things that require you to be available at all times…. But the reality is that these things generally don't move as quickly as people predict they're going to move.

McCollum also told of an unspoken rule in her division that full-time lawyers get the "million-dollar cases" and other high-visibility assignments, which give them recognition. McCollum believes her "high turnover of half-million-dollar cases, which add up" should give her skills some visibility as well, and make her eligible for further challenging work.

Leadership roles on cases are also denied to part-time attorneys. In government, for example, where projects tend to be handled by teams of lawyers, part-timers find it difficult to demonstrate their supervisory skills and management potential. According to Lorna Michaelson, who was resigned to playing a subordinate role to full-time colleagues on joint projects:

You can't be the lead person on a lot of issues. Smaller issues, yes. Things where you're doing general counseling, giving advice…. But in terms of being able to take a leadership position…you lose out on that.

When part-time lawyers are given opportunities to work on more complex and challenging cases and to exercise leadership, it is usually because a supervisor or partner has intervened in some way or has made a special request.

Lateral hiring: As law firms, corporations, and government agencies hire lawyers from the outside more and more to fill positions requiring expertise in specialty areas, many part-timers find that there is no clear career-tracking system.

Patricia Bianchini, a part-time staff attorney who had been a litigator with a government agency for 10 years, reported that until recently there was no chance for mobility in her organization because top administrators had held their jobs for so long. On their retirement, mobility possibilities did not improve, however, because the search for replacements was conducted outside the department, with negative consequences for part-time attorneys. Moreover, when the new, laterally hired managers have not worked with a lawyer before she or he became part time, they lack an institutional memory of the person's contributions.

Mentorship: As in all fields, mentorship is vital to advancement in the legal profession (Epstein, 1970; Epstein *et al.*, 1995). This is especially true in private law firms and in corporations, where advocacy by senior partners and corporate officers is often a decisive factor in promotion decisions. In the role of mentor, senior lawyers offer sponsorship by recommending junior colleagues for special assignments; they provide opportunities for protégés and their work to be showcased to influential partners or executives, thus helping them to establish good reputations. According to Christina Weatherspoon, an associate practicing environmental law at an eminent Wall Street firm, "You have to be known by all the partners to become a partner." Ultimately, the mentor who has watched over and guided the steps of a junior colleague acts as advocate for his or her protégé during the promotion process.

Some lawyers find it difficult to start or sustain relationships with mentors when they move to part-time work. When they go off the full-time track, they lose access to informal networks. The following comment by Constance Crane, who over the course of many years at a large corporate firm did develop strong mentorship bonds, describes how partners withdrew from her when she went part-time:

> One partner would say to me, "Look, you're not treated any different than someone who isn't going to make partner." Once you're sort of off the track—in their mind or in reality—they don't focus on you, you know?... [They stop] paying attention to you, grooming you. And getting good deals and mentoring you and making sure you're included.

Women partners, according to Crane, are just as unavailable as male partners for mentoring to part-time attorneys. In her view this occurs for reasons that are emotionally loaded:

> There is a lot of tension at [the firm] between the female partners...who do not have it all—who have the career, who are very much opposed to part time, or very much don't want to help you have it all. "You can't have it all. I couldn't have it all. I made my choice. You have to make your choice." Really, [they] go out of their way to not help you.... I think they're jealous.... They gave up having a family. And, yeah, I think it's total jealousy.

While this image of the childless, family-free female partner as resentful and withholding toward junior colleagues has been noted in previous accounts of generational frictions between women lawyers, it stereotypes and distorts the facts. Our study of corporate law firms (Epstein *et al.*, 1995) found that most women partners in the firms studied are married (73 percent) and about the same percentage have children.[55] Some women partners doubtless display ambivalence about becoming advocates for part-time women, but what is often labeled as personal insensitivity can be as easily explained by their structural positions within their firms. Severe time constraints, low seniority, and the lack of power they wield make mentoring difficult. The small number of women partners in most firms means that many are "tokens" with an attendant symbolic responsibility to represent women as a group—a role not conducive to individual advising and advocacy (Epstein *et al.*, 1995: 350–351; Kanter, 1977). The stereotype of the "martyred" female partner is tenacious, however, as illustrated by Constance Crane's comment above. Yet in another part of her interview Crane recalled being given the opportunity to gain trial experience by a woman partner, and the experience challenged her assumptions about female partners' failure to support younger women lawyers:

> She thought it would be difficult for me to get trial experience here because the kind of trials we do are 24-hour—when we get to that point, which we often don't...it's overwhelming.... So she thought that this was the best way for me to get trial experience.
>
> •   •   •
>
> It was nice of her to think of me. Particularly being a woman who has opted not to have children, to put her career first.... That is opposed to what you hear a lot of times—that women [who] are successful think, "I don't have what you have, and therefore, you can't have what I have." She didn't do that to me, which I appreciated.

Informal relations at work: As discussed in greater detail in Chapter 11, socializing with colleagues—another source of informal networking that can affect advancement—is also more problematic for part-time lawyers. Information is often exchanged and camaraderie reinforced over lunch or drinks. Part-time lawyers report they are more likely to eat lunch at their desks rather than use the time to cultivate social ties with colleagues, and they rarely join colleagues after work for drinks. Their "efficient" methods of using work time do not allow them to leave their desks or offices for the informal exchanges that create ties useful in making connections.

Although it is a highly subjective aspect of the promotion equation, the extent to which a lawyer "fits" with the style and culture of the organization is continually evaluated by heads of law firms, in-house law departments, and government legal divisions. A person's willingness to "shmooze"[56] with colleagues and attend social functions becomes a measure of organizational dedication and commitment.

Not having time to socialize with colleagues was seen to be a career barrier by a number of part-time attorneys. Susannah Lukens, a biochemist turned lawyer working at a management consulting company, remarked that she did not believe that her telecommuting arrangement itself undermined her chances of becoming partner as much as her lack of involvement in the social life of her company.

Business development (rainmaking): The proven ability or perceived potential of individual lawyers to generate business is a major factor in many partnership decisions as firms become increasingly preoccupied with bottom-line concerns. In this situation—unique to private law firms—part-time lawyers find themselves at a disadvantage, since "rainmaking" activities typically require after-work meetings with prospective clients as well as appearances at professional events and social affairs. At the same time, some firms have promoted part-time lawyers specifically because they have been able to bring the business of a major client to the firm. Justine Grimshaw identified what she believed was the overriding agenda at her former firm when it came to partnership decisions:

> Excellent work is excellent work. But when it comes to partnership positions, there will probably be a detriment [to those who fail to produce business development]. [Partners would say,] "Why should we be sharing our partnership...with someone who's not as committed, even if they do excellent work?" ... [Nevertheless] things are changing at big firms.... Now business is business. And if you've got clients, you've got money coming in, there's a lot more leeway given for different lifestyles, different attitudes.

Julia Fine, an international trade specialist who left a position as a part-time partner to take an in-house job, lamented the difficulty of finding time to engage in rainmaking activities in her firm:

> As a junior partner you were expected to develop business. And clearly nobody stays in a partnership unless they bring in their own clients and continue to sustain themselves.... You have to go out.... I was on panels and giving speeches and writing articles. That happens *after* you do your work.... If you were going to go anywhere, if you were going to go the next step [to equity partner] you'd have to start spending a lot more time rainmaking.

Professional development: Reduced opportunity for professional development is a natural and inevitable consequence of part-time legal practice. Part-time lawyers may reduce participation in bar association activities and may even cut back professional reading. Such limitations were articulated by Philipa Kasinetz, a recently laid-off part-time in-house staff attorney. She noted the difficulty of fitting in all the extra time demands made by meetings and seminars:

> One of the problems that I found...we would have [continuing legal education] seminars in-house which were not mandatory, but—the general counsel would go, or the assistant general—you wanted to be seen there.... They were always on a Thursday which is my day off.... I had to keep my hours, I had to read the periodicals [and other] stuff in three-fifths [time].... There's much more play if you work full time—you can fit it in.

Compromised career growth is an outcome of curtailing outside professional activities.

Aging Out

Some of the senior attorneys interviewed for the study expressed a two-fold concern about the impact of their long-term part-time status on their chances to find work congruent with their experience and expectations for high rank. They worry, first that they have been part time too long to be considered seriously for full-time jobs and, second that they are thought to be too old or too set in their ways to be valuable and too "over-the-hill" for a position of the rank they are qualified for.

Part-time work takes lawyers' careers "off-schedule," or at least off any schedule an attorney would consider to be reasonable. Individuals who do not succeed in a career by the time or stage in life in which success is expected to occur—thus deviating from "career timetables" (Roth, 1963)—may be labeled failures (Levin and Levin, 1991).[57] These timetables include a series of stages or phases leading to a goal or end point. Developing a professional career, individuals are expected to move from entry-level positions to midlevel managerial positions, and finally to assume managerial and executive titles, a "status-sequence," according to Robert K. Merton (1957). Those who fall outside of the expected trajectory are seen to be off-schedule, and, as a result, may be treated as time deviants (Byrne, 1988; Zerubavel, 1981); and like other deviants, they may find their behavior negatively sanctioned.

The consequences of career immobility in a firm are captured by the comment of Charlotte Smith, an in-house attorney:

Most of my friends had left or were in partnership positions, which separated [me] from the rest...[it was] a real division.

Part-Time Lawyers Remove Themselves from a Mobility Track

A number of part-time lawyers drop out of the running for advancement. June Vaughn, a part-time associate at a large firm, told us how she enviously watched members of her class advance to partner while her career dreams diminished. She described her mind-set at the moment:

I [have] an employee mentality. I do this work...very well. But [unlike the others] I don't ask, "When are the new cases coming in? I want a piece of that,"...and that's the kind of thing you should do if you want to become a partner.

Stephanie Joran, another part-time associate, expressed a similar sentiment, "I'm not sure I have a career. I have a job. A career has a future and a path. I'm not sure I have a path."

Not only are these professionals' ambitions downscaled, but their willingness to pursue challenging work and responsibility has been damaged by the frustration of performing work with uncertain levels of backup and lack of recognition. Although many part-time lawyers claim to have phases when they work considerably more than their agreed hours, they often feel that if they do not watch the boundaries, the firm or legal department for which they work would violate them. We heard a common complaint that organizations would squeeze as much work out of an attorney as they could. Many lawyers said they felt they were on a slippery slope and feared their part-time schedules could creep back to full time.

Hence, part-time attorneys face ambivalence about how much responsibility they wish to have. On the one hand, many express a desire to be assigned to meaty cases—the interesting ones with high visibility. At the same time they know that taking them may cause them to work beyond their desired schedule and may not lead to increased recognition or status.

Factors Contributing to Advancement: Situations in Which Mobility Is Possible

Mobility is by no means impossible for part-time attorneys, although the rate of career progress generally is slower than for full-timers, and the type of progress may be different. Despite the obstacles, some structural and cultural conditions and strategic choices support mobility. A substantial number of lawyers interviewed for the study—many of them formerly part-time—have had mobility. A small number advanced while they were part-time; some were promoted after resuming full-time schedules; some were permitted to have part-time schedules after achieving partnership; and a larger number of lawyers advanced by moving laterally from one firm to another or to an in-house position. Though these lateral moves did not necessarily lead to a higher rank, they resulted in improved work conditions. Some attorneys alternated between full-time and part-time work, moving upward and downward.

We interviewed a few lawyers who held part-time partnerships, but these cases seemed idiosyncratic to their personal situations. In one case, the lawyer had a strong personal tie to the firm's leading client; in another, the attorney worked in a firm where a precedent was set by a woman partner who had negotiated a part-time position after many years as a full-time partner. In both cases the attorneys worked 80 to 90 percent of full-time and drew appropriate reduced partnership income shares.

Thus part-time status does not necessarily block an attorney's career. It may impose some kind of ceiling or slow it down, or force relocation to another organization or sphere. And in a few individual cases, a person's excellence or connection with powerful clients may open channels not available for most others.

Searching for patterns in the careers of part-time lawyers who attained some type of mobility we found these:

Culture, competition, and opportunity structures: Geographic location matters. Only 2.1 percent of lawyers in large New York law firms work part time; firms in other cities are somewhat more receptive to it (*National Law Journal,* Feb. 6, 1995; *Wall Street Journal,* Feb. 24, 1995). Pockets of opportunity may be found in some regions, although some reports indicate that firms in San Francisco, Los Angeles, Washington, and Chicago are becoming like New York. Ninety-five percent of law firms in San Francisco grant part-time work, and 4.2 percent of their lawyers take it. In Washington, D.C., 90 percent of firms grant these schedules, and only 2.8 percent of lawyers take them.

Firms that are innovative in other spheres seem more receptive to reduced hours. For example, in California's Silicon Valley, five successful women partners in high-tech law firms of more than 100 attorneys, profiled in *The California Lawyer* (Beck, 1997), were described as having educated themselves in the basics of computer hardware, software programming, semiconductor production, and the Internet to deal with practices handling high-tech mergers and acquisitions and doing basic corporate and securities work for start-ups. They included Diane Savage, of Cooley, Godward, Castro, Huddleson, and Tatum, the mother of three children, who had worked part time (60 to 80 percent) for 16 years as an associate and as a partner. (Part-time meant 8 a.m. to 6 p.m., five days a week.) Stacy Snowman's 30-lawyer products, technology, and multimedia group at Gray, Cary, Ware and Freidenrich included four part-timers, including one male attorney.[58]

Firms that do not have constant quick-turnaround pressures also are more receptive to part-timers' advancement. In addition, a few part-time lawyers in our study who worked for the federal government were led to believe that their chances for advancement might be better in smaller cities.

Specialization: The cultivation of legal specialties creates a pathway to lateral and upward mobility, providing an extra element of "human capital" (Gary Becker, 1976; Bourdieu, [1972], 1977) that enhances the value of part-timers and cancels some of the stigma attached to reduced hours. The career trajectories of a handful of lawyers—particularly those in private law firms—demonstrate that having expertise in tax or securities law, or specialties such as alternative dispute resolution, or familiarity with the needs of high-tech companies can be especially important in negotiating part-time status. For Nicole Leon Welch, a part-time partner, developing a niche in a specialized area of law was meant to "rehabilitate the perceptions" of her as "less than serious."

By strategically developing expertise, lawyers use their knowledge and skills to leverage more desirable career arrangements. There is common understanding that the professional relationship is an exchange relationship (Homans, 1961), and that the perceived cost of part-time status to an institution can be offset by the value added by an attorney's expertise and specialization (and reduced compensation).

Some of the specialties of part-time attorneys tend to be in service areas at law firms—say, a specialty that augments a major transaction or real estate deal. Tax lawyers, for example, usually work on cases brought in by other attorneys, and their work often focuses on a piece of a larger matter.

With encouragement from mentors, one associate in a large firm learned state securities law to develop a "nice little niche." This was a key factor in her ability to change from working full-time in one large firm to working part-time in another. She thought it gave her added bargaining power in the process of negotiating the arrangement.

Expertise in an area of foreign law and debt was helpful for another attorney, who had been encouraged by her mentor to specialize so she could be hired as a consultant to a firm on a limited basis.

A very well-seasoned attorney with a thriving practice, Joelle Neuman, described her strategy of developing a new niche/specialty area of law as a route to making a place for herself within the partnership. But she expressed frustration at the apparently gendered nature of the pressures that led her to do it:

How many men have to do that [develop a specialty] to become a partner when they've proven that they're qualified to do the work, basically?

Such strategies could backfire, however. Neuman pointed out one draw-back to developing a practice area new to the firm: It left her without major partners to back her for partnership. Given the politics of partnership decis-ions, partners were more likely to vie for partners in their practice group.

Having a specialty legal practice expedited the negotiation of alternative employment arrangements in-house and in the government, although it was less common than in firms. In one case, an attorney was able to work out a part-time consultant status with a title of special counsel, unusual since the acquisition of a title that expresses an attorney's seniority and rank is difficult to obtain.

Many attorneys interviewed for this study viewed law firms as providing greater opportunities for advancement than either the legal departments of corporations or the government. They argued that in corporations and the government, career chances are more or less fixed (or predictable). Opportunities in government agencies are limited by politically set budgets. In-house attorneys face flat hierarchies in legal departments; promotion often entails moving to a managerial position elsewhere in the company in a non-legal role. In law firms, however, lawyers have seen that those who bring in clients and are perceived as potential assets to the partnership's business devel-opment concerns can make partner—whether or not such openings formally exist. Opportunity grows to accommodate the lucrative prospects of rainmak-ers, as Lydia Churchill, an in-house lawyer, observed:

There's not a lot of room for advancement in-house.... When you're in a law firm—if you want to advance, you go out and get more clients.... And if you...bring in the clients, you have power.

Proving themselves: Although women attorneys continue to have to prove themselves (Epstein, [1981] 1993), part-timers especially feel they have to do it to justify the special accommodation of the reduced hours given them.

Elinor Parker, a full-time government attorney who had been part-time for a number of years, was eager to apply for a supervisory position. Parker told how a senior colleague discouraged her from pursuing the position because there was a period of "make-up time" that she would have to serve before being considered for promotion. How much time was necessary, however, was unclear; as she and others saw it, "I just don't know how long that effect [of having been part-time] will linger."

In another case, Tracy Long, a part-time in-house attorney at a large communications company, was cautioned by her mentor about obstacles she would have to surmount before she could hope to be perceived as fit for promotion to the vice president's position she sought:

> [My mentor said], "I don't think you [will get] that job so easily because there is a taint.... You worked part-time for a few years...a burden that you have to overcome."

The taint, of course, was the perception that reduced hours meant a reduced commitment. As the mentor analyzed the situation:

> I think it goes to commitment—a perceived lack of commitment to your employer.... I think what you would need to do is come back to work full-time, take the management training course, kick ass for a while, show them you are really back and ready to work full time, and then after you do that for a while, then you will be taken seriously.

Having taken part-time work for a year after her first child was born, a return to full-time work at the beginning of her second pregnancy was an important symbolic step for Susan Zukin. It demonstrated her commitment, and she ultimately became a partner in the firm.

Flexibility: Child-care arrangements are tied into the economic and cultural ethos of family and work. Lawyers with high incomes can afford child care that is highly flexible in meeting the demands of the workplace. Others with high incomes feel that a rigid schedule without flexibility is better for maintaining a boundary between work and parenting. Lawyers with more modest incomes are often limited in their ability to afford child care except when they are actually at work. This is most feasible when they work for the government or another sector with fixed hours and predictable schedules. Certainly, lawyers who can rise to a crisis and work at unscheduled times are more likely to be regarded as committed and ambitious and to have more opportunity to rise in their organizations.

Thus, we see the road to serious career advancement in the legal profession is hampered by part-time work schedules. However, some mobility is possible if supervisors who make evaluations are positive about the potential of part-time lawyers and recognize their contributions, and if the lawyers themselves are flexible and responsive to the needs of their organizations.

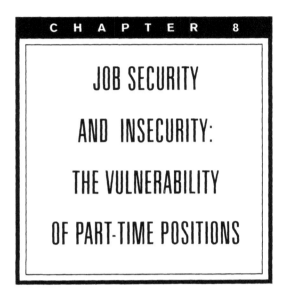

CHAPTER 8

JOB SECURITY AND INSECURITY: THE VULNERABILITY OF PART-TIME POSITIONS

The legal profession has endured violent turbulence in the last decade. Several old, established corporate law firms have disbanded, among them Mudge, Rose, Guthrie, Alexander and Ferdon, Richard Nixon's law firm. Other leading corporate firms have faced serious competition for their clients. Government legal offices and corporation legal departments have been downsized. When business declines, as it did in the early 1990s, part-time attorneys are especially vulnerable. Several of the lawyers interviewed recalled a time in the recent past when everyone working part-time in one large legal department was fired. Thus part-timers are caught in a trap: they wish to work fewer hours but are aware that their status makes them especially vulnerable and exposed. This predicament puts pressure on many to work beyond their agreed-upon hours.

This situation was described by a Meredith Lewis, who recalled how she and her job-share partner took on a large workload in the first year of their newly pioneered arrangement. Although their arrangement was planned to give them both reduced hours, Lewis and her partner were afraid to turn back any of the work, despite the fact that they were given permission by management to do so. As she explained:

> In a corporation your work is your security, and so we were hesitant to give it up....The way to survive in the corporate legal department is to have a lot of work.

To minimize the chances of being left with too few clients and thus being perceived as superfluous, Linda Lofland, a no-nonsense in-house attorney on a flexible time schedule, developed a strategy to keep control of her practice. Lofland carves out specialized work with clients so that she is not dependent on other lawyers to give her work. In this way she bypasses the assignment procedures—which she believes would otherwise result in a workload reduction. Her clients seek her out directly or specifically ask for her to serve as their lawyer.

Oddly enough, at least one part-time attorney found opportunity—an unanticipated if short-term consequence—in the demise of her company. Lydia Fiske was able to negotiate a part-time arrangement because the company was in liquidation, and it made economic sense to keep her on in a limited capacity. The other lawyers were fired but she was retained because the organization could more easily exploit a part-timer than they could a full-time person.

Lack of "Place"

The lack of legitimate status in itself appears to give rise to job insecurity among part-timers because it symbolizes the fact that there is no permanent place in the organizational hierarchy or plan for them. It highlights the fact that part-time lawyers are regarded as transients—particularly in law firms and corporations, though to a lesser extent in the government.

In an image that came up repeatedly in our interviews, part-timers "are neither fish nor fowl." At her yearly evaluation, one attorney remarked, she was reminded that her choice to work as a part-time associate was perceived as a stopgap measure with no permanence in the firm's structure:

> [The partner said,] "How long do you think you're going to do this?" First question. So it's not, "Oh...we're so happy this is working out great." [What this means is] that part-time isn't a...way of life. It is a short-term answer to the problem of having small children.... If I'm serious about staying here—you are an associate, or you are a partner....There is not a ton of in-between. And...there are no part-time partners.

Commenting on the precariousness of her part-time associate position in a large firm, Rosalind Mei said that the partners send a message: that they are "willing to keep good people around forever," but as a part-timer, "I am vulnerable.... The joke is that after you get your review, you get another six months tenure."

Because in most organizations part-time attorneys are off-track, they are more vulnerable to layoffs. Sheila Reinhardt, a government attorney, explained that in her office a person who shifts from full-time to part-time relinquishes seniority during the reduced schedule. A relatively recent part-timer with many years of full-time service could be laid off before a full-time attorney with fewer years of service. However, she pointed out, under certain circumstances part-timers may revert to full-time status and resume their previous seniority ranking. This possibility is, of course, available only to government attorneys, not to those in law firms or corporate legal departments.

Part-time partners are vulnerable to layoffs if they do not have a strong client base. There is an illusory security to achieving partnership, we learned. Having recently become a part-time partner, Florence Whorf said she feels she may be "kicked out" of the firm if she decides to have a second child.

Layoffs

Seven of the attorneys we interviewed for this study were laid off from their jobs in government and corporations. Although most lost their jobs through company mergers or changes in political administrations that led to cuts in full-time staff, part-time lawyers were often the first to go. As one former in-house attorney put it, "I think that I probably went to the front of the list."

Imagining the logic that her company probably used to make decisions about layoffs during a recent merger that left her (and all but one of her part-time colleagues) unemployed, Joanna Kay reasoned:

> It probably wasn't the biggest leap in the world to say, "Well, if we could do without them [the part-timers] one or two days a week we could do without them for four or five days a week." You know, "We could do without them the whole time."

Part-time lawyers are more vulnerable to layoffs in part because they are perceived as having a looser connection to the work community than those who work full-time, and thus managers feel less obligated to protect them. In terms of the unstated social contract, letting part-timers go first seems fair. Furthermore, the disempowering aspects of part-timers' status undercuts their value because they tend to work on lower-profile cases and have weak ties to partners or key managers who might serve as advocates during times of organizational transition. Far from holding a pollyannaish view about organizational politics, Joyce Rhode had a hunch about her company's downsizing plan that suggests she saw the handwriting on the wall:

> I wasn't particularly political; nobody who was in a position to help me knew what I was doing.... When the merger happened...budgets had to be cut, people had to be axed, who was important, who wasn't, who's high profile, who wasn't.... My sense [was] throughout—I said it early on, "You watch, all the part-timers are going to be gone."

Fairness and Job Security

Opinions vary as to whether it is fair for part-time lawyers to be more vulnerable to job loss than their full-time counterparts. At one firm, when a spate of firings of part-time associates was repeatedly brought up, a managing partner linked his decision to the vicissitudes of corporate practice:

> When things slowed down, the people who worked part-time and filled gaps in the workload were no longer needed. For the rest [working] on transactions... days don't pass where you aren't needed. Often that includes weekends.... It's really a seven-day-a-week job, and it would be very difficult to make it a three-day-a-week job.

In contrast, Connie Trent, a recently fired in-house attorney, had a very different opinion. She was cynical about official rationales, believing that part-time lawyers—if valued—could be retained:

> They say, "Your position's being eliminated." But it's really a bunch of baloney.... If they wanted me, they would have said, "Connie, this is the situation: You can't stay part-time, [but]... we want you to stay and [we'll work out another situation]."

Institutional Differences in Job Security

Corporation in-house attorneys interviewed for our study were more susceptible to layoffs than those in the government or in law firms. As we have noted, this may be because there has been so much downsizing of managerial and administrative ranks, the category into which lawyers fall. Further, organizational shifts that lead to layoffs of lawyers vary by institution, and industry probably has weaker allegiances to its lawyers than do law firms. When law firms merge, for example, partners tend to shepherd their practice groups to the new firm intact. Two part-time lawyers in our study benefited from mergers because their status was regarded as an economic benefit. This stands in contrast to the typical fallout from mergers in corporations, in which part-time employees and others regarded as not meeting the productivity standard are phased out.

Government attorneys have most protection because of personnel regulations enforcing seniority. However, changes in political administrations can wipe out entire offices.

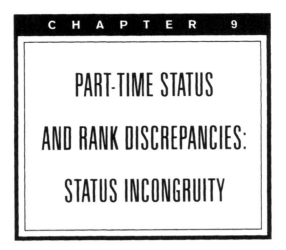

C H A P T E R   9

PART-TIME STATUS AND RANK DISCREPANCIES: STATUS INCONGRUITY

The Dilemmas and Contradictions of Status Discrepancies

Status contradictions are a major concern of part-time lawyers.[59] For example, in private law firms, seasoned associates with histories of full-time work would qualify for senior rank if they had not chosen part-time schedules. It is common, especially in large firms, for senior associates, even those who are on a part-time schedule, to supervise junior colleagues and to have direct contact with longstanding clients. Yet, most part-timers are usually limited to the entry-level title of "associate" in large firms, no matter what their responsibilities. Similarly, part-time attorneys who are assistant general counsels in industry and staff attorneys in government may not have titles that characterize their skills and experience. Put succinctly by one discouraged part-timer, "There's no recognition for the seniority and the confidence that you have."

The discrepancies among experience, age, and official status create two interrelated types of difficulties for part-time lawyers and the organizations that employ them. The first is the diminishing esteem many part-time lawyers experience because they do not obtain the usual symbolic markers of seniority and the prestige that goes with them. The second is clients' perceptions that they have or will have limited or poorer service from part-time lawyers, and the potential for client development that is undermined when a client's lawyers do not possess high rank.

Status discrepancies also create unease when colleagues find it awkward to interact with individuals who may evoke contradictory norms related to their differently ranked statuses. For example, being senior in an organization commands respect. But being senior in age and experience but holding a junior rank and being subordinate to a younger boss causes discomfort.

Consequences for Personal and Professional Identity

Part-timers who are senior in age and low in rank perceive themselves as standing still, in a "holding pattern"; "still an associate after all those years," as one attorney put it. By and large, the organizational charts of laws firms, companies, and government agencies do not have titles that distinguish senior part-time attorneys from their less experienced colleagues, thus condemning part-timers to prestige limbo.[60]

Without proper status recognition, part-timers can fall through organizational cracks and become professionally invisible. Nancy Brown, an attorney in a midtown firm, said of her lack of a sense of place: "Because you're part-time...you're sort of nowheres-ville."

The structural ambiguity that comes from being out of step with the usual sequence in which a person moves through organizational hierarchies with a career timetable hurts lawyers' professional esteem and morale, particularly when it is coupled with self-consciousness about age. Resentment and a sense of disgrace was expressed by part-time attorneys as they watched younger, junior colleagues surpass them in rank.

Status and age issues were pivotal for Carol Grant, a part-time attorney in her late 30s, who contemplated pursuing part-time work at a large firm but who ultimately rejected it for a part-time position in a corporation.

> The lack of status is something that I really struggle with.... As I looked at this new job...I thought, "Do I really want to go be an associate?"...The people that I was interviewing with who are partners are six years younger than I am.... They're all going to make a million dollars and they want to pay me this piddling salary?... Is that really going to be comfortable?... I have these great credentials, and I deserve to reap the benefits of them...and part of the benefit is making it and reaping financial rewards and status.

The social awkwardness of status and age discrepancies is experienced by part-timers when they find themselves reporting to "greener" attorneys as status equals. Barbara Jennings, a 42-year-old 17th-year associate who was unsuccessful in negotiating a title that reflected her seniority, reported:

> [I walked] into a partner's office yesterday and looked at him, [and thought] "Is he 12 yet?" [He was so] very young looking and in fact, very young—35 years old....

You look and you say, "This is a partner and I'm not.".... It gets a little hard going to the printers [an associate's job] as I do with 23-year-olds and 24-year-olds. And being the old lady in the room.[61]

The Gender Factor

Because a majority of part-time lawyers are women, who often have problems establishing their authority under the best of circumstances, rank discrepancies add to their struggle for recognition and respect. Karen Forbes, a part-time lawyer in a firm described it:

> When my class first reached [the partnership stage], three or four years ago, [being part-time] wasn't a problem. Now that I've been practicing 12 years it becomes more of a problem.... I just got off a deal...with a younger man in his early 30s. He is a very kind of Mr. Macho kind of guy—into the guys, very into status. On top of the fact that I was a woman, I also wasn't a partner, and so he had a lot of difficulty dealing with me.

Status discrepancies can widen the gender gap among lawyers within organizations, as the largely part-time women idle in status while men bound ahead.

Effects of Discrepant Statuses on Clients' Perceptions of Competence

Further consequences of status discrepancies flow from clients' perceptions of the service they receive from part-time attorneys. Does the fact that an attorney has not been promoted in several years send a negative message to clients about the quality of the attorney assigned to them and of the work they are getting? Joshua Taylor, a partner at a large firm whose elegant designer-decorated corner office indicated the importance of his firm's symbol of rank, said he thinks clients care about the status of the attorneys who work on their cases. "Having the title makes a difference in terms of client perception of you and your own perception of yourself," he said.

Other attorneys registered concern about clients' perceptions. Many part-time associates who were very senior felt it was necessary to explain to clients (as well as to colleagues outside their division) why they were still associates.

Gina Paolucci, an attorney who specializes in environmental litigation and works in a city agency, also felt she owed her clients an explanation about why she was not being promoted to a supervisory position despite her five years of experience. Several of them had known her long enough to be aware of the fact that she has not moved up with her group. An off-schedule attorney, she wanted to mitigate the stigma of being a "time deviant" and create a better impression for clients who may perceive part-time lawyers without prestigious titles as being second rank:

> I feel I want them to know I'm really a smart person.... I really *would* have a title if I wasn't part time. I think a title is a big thing... I feel like an explanation is always due to the people that I'm working with and why I don't have a title.

Consequences of Title Devaluation for Organizational Image

Law firms and other organizations may unwittingly punish themselves by keeping their experienced part-time lawyers in low-ranking titles. Two of the attorneys interviewed suggested that offering experienced part-time attorneys higher-level titles could be beneficial to the public relations efforts of law firms without incurring any real costs. Lisa Mulligan, a part-time associate in the real estate department of a large Wall Street firm, somewhat cynically suggested that her firm could improve its image by granting senior titles to part-timers, creating the appearance that it had a better record promoting women than was actually the case:

> [The managing partner doesn't] believe in [the title of] "part-time counsel." He was talking about the disparity in ratios [between] male to female partners.... So I joked, "Well, if you make me counsel, that would help."

Creating titles that reflect rank and seniority could also be important for rainmaking. As we learned from some attorneys at large firms, it could send a message to potential clients that the firm is healthy enough to be promoting people—that is, even if there were no other tangible rewards connected to offering part-timers higher-level titles.

Of course, the discrepant statuses that part-time lawyers develop and the discomfort it causes them serve to hold most lawyers to a standard of full-time work. Since the discrepancy can only get worse as they age professionally, this also motivates attorneys to limit the duration of their part-time tenure.

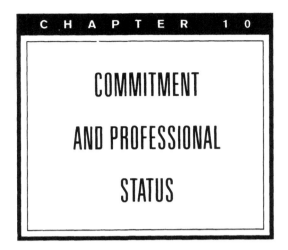

CHAPTER 10

COMMITMENT

AND PROFESSIONAL

STATUS

Part-time lawyers find that attributes and qualities that have nothing to do with the number of hours they work are called into question. Like blind people who are not regarded to be as intelligent as those who are sighted, part-timers may be regarded as being less commited than full-timers (Goffman, 1963). Indeed, they may even question this quality themselves. Organizations prize commitment and look for ways to identify it. Limiting the number of hours devoted to work is thought to signal a lack of devotion to the organization's goals, and often such attorneys are seen as not being "real professionals." Part-time status thus may become a proxy for low commitment (or lack of excellence).

Commitment is an important element in the "norm of reciprocity" (Gouldner, 1960) between lawyers and managers or partners in the professional settings in which they work. We have seen that lawyers are supposed to show commitment by the time they put in, and in return, the professional organization is expected to grant opportunity, job continuity, and autonomy. This ideal has been undermined in recent years through changes in the legal profession, but, nevertheless, it remains a standard.

Thus part-time attorneys' commitments are a concern. Although many part-timers do feel committed, many agree that their part-time status is an indicator of less commitment than full-timers demonstrate. Some colleagues acknowledge that part-timers may have high commitment, but a larger number believe they do not.

The issue of commitment is not synonymous with excellence, but it is related to it. Many part-timers are known to be good workers. Indeed, as we noted earlier, it is usually the experienced performers who are granted part-time assignments. Nonetheless, their devotion to career becomes questioned because they do not put in the overtime hours taken for granted by those who identify with the organization and hope to rise within it.

In most sectors of the law but especially in private firms there is a concern that part-timers will not contribute to the common enterprise by developing business or engaging in its training functions. The limit on hours means that the part-time attorney may not complete assigned tasks and thus may create extra work for full-time lawyers. Although not all full-time attorneys conform to the idealized view of total commitment, the reduced schedules of the part-time attorneys are assessed—and usually found deficient—against a norm of total dedication.

Because this norm defines the "professional," it is widely held both by attorneys at the top of the hierarchy and those subordinate to them. Many part-timers accept that they will face limits on professional mobility as part of the cost of working part time. In fact, those who do become partners (a very small proportion of them) encounter confusion because that status is typically granted only to those regarded as the most committed professionals, and they do not fit the ideal. Rose Gladstone, an associate at a midtown firm that expanded rapidly during the 1980s, described the reaction of colleagues and clients to part-time partners:

> I think it's confusing to people to be committed and be a partner—but be part time. They don't know which camp you fall in.

The confusion over "which camp" a part-time partner falls into is not merely personal. An attorney's place in the firm has multiple meanings. Partnership signals to those inside and outside the firm a level of commitment, skill, power, and social networks greater than that of an associate. The composite of attributes defines the desired "partner."

Impact on Lawyers' Self-Concepts

The relationship between the normative standards of the profession and individual lawyers' evaluations of themselves is interactive (Markus et al., 1997).[62] Lawyers internalize standards of commitment. We found that some attorneys we interviewed were quite harsh with themselves and expressed self-doubts about their role as a professional. They become ambivalent about their performance and question their worth. Harriet Jones, a former part-time consultant, echoed the sentiments of many other part-time attorneys in recalling her guilty feelings of not measuring up to

> a professional standard that professional self-worth should be measured by constant availability, desire for partnership, and doing "sexy" deals.

The Norm of Reciprocity and the Issue of Commitment

Yet there are holes in the normative structure that determines the patterns of commitment today. The norm of reciprocity (Gouldner, 1960)—reciprocity from the top down as well as from the bottom up—has become problematic, and lawyers no longer feel confident that firms can be trusted to reciprocate for their dedication.[63] In the past, firms and corporations could be counted on to offer loyal and committed professionals job tenure. Even with an "up or out" policy,[64] jobs with corporate clients were usually found for associates when they failed to attain partnership. Because chances for partnership have become slimmer and clients less reliable, it often happens today that neither promotion nor alternative employment can be offered, and job security is diminished. The lack of fit between employer guarantees and employee loyalty and the growing contingency of jobs has been labeled "loose coupling" by sociologists (DiTomaso, 1996). It would seem, therefore, that employers would come to realize they cannot ask for the same level of employee commitment they could expect in the past. Nevertheless, employers do desire employee commitment, and because they have the power to create schedules and offer whatever mobility there is in the system, the norms are maintained without reciprocal loyalties, but the new dynamic is perceived as unfair and exploitative.

Job security for lawyers, whether full time or part time, differs among the sectors of law. In the past, large corporate law firms constituted the most precarious environments because of their slim chances for promotion to partnership. In New York, between 10 percent and 20 percent of associates are elevated to partners (Epstein *et al.,* 1995; Galanter and Palay, 1991), although in most the figure runs closer to one in 10. But lawyers working in these firms hope to make partner, even against the odds. Changes in other sectors have also made many lawyers apprehensive about their futures. Programs such as the Clinton administration's "Reinventing Government" have mandated cuts in government agencies. Corporations have downsized both professional and managerial ranks. Thus the "socially expected duration" (Merton, 1984) of employment tenure and mobility does not reflect the actual duration of work life in a firm, or in the other sectors of the law, or the duration expected today.

In law firms, therefore, partners may use negative assessments of "commitment" as tools to justify lower expectations of employer obligation and to "cool out" (Goffman, [1952] 1980) younger lawyers who might have aimed high without conforming to the ideal norms.

Many younger attorneys do not have a realistic picture of the inequities, or do not accept the time commitment demanded as a measure of professionalism. So it may be true that a proportion of lawyers are not committed according to the standard imposed—that is, that all their other roles are subordinated to their professional role. After all, most part-time lawyers are mothers whose dedication to family and children competes with their dedication to work.

Part-time lawyers may be quite devoted to their work as well as to their families, and may work hard at their jobs and aspire to achieve the rewards of experience and seniority later in their lives. But many attorneys seemed defensive about these choices and judgments. As a part-time partner in a small firm, where she felt the full-time partners did not give her the respect she deserved, Janet Fried acknowledged that she has a reduced commitment when measured in hours, but she feels it is not a "forever choice." She resented her partners for not having a longer view of her career commitment.

The Argument for Commitment

With changing ideology in the profession, some lawyers believe the legal workplace and its norms should change and that part-time work ought not to constrain advancement. They do not see time as a proxy for commitment or excellence. Peggy Garity, a part-time seventh-year associate in a high-profile firm, reasoned that it was illogical for colleagues to regard part-timers as uncommitted. She pointed out that women want part-time work so that they can both further their careers and have children, not because they want to ease out of the profession or lightly invest themselves in a career. She argued against the lore that women lawyers have the attitude that they will develop careers and then opt out when they have children, and that they are not interested in career satisfaction:

> There are very few people, very few women, who have this attitude of, "I'm just going to keep working less and less and ease myself out."... That's counter-intuitive to me.... If you don't want to work and want to be home with your kids, then you leave. [So] if you [are] working, then you *want* to be working.

> •   •   •

> If you invested in a law degree and have been in this fast-paced environment, your idea of a great time isn't doing busywork and sliding out the door at the end of the day.... It's no fun coming into a job that you know has absolutely no future to it.... To the extent that women...leave altogether, it's probably more because

they're thoroughly disgruntled and demoralized than it is that they lose their will to work.

Sara Atwater, a full-time partner in a downtown firm who had been a part-time associate, was sensitive to the constant awareness and assessment of availability part-time lawyers felt. She agreed that part-timers were regarded as less committed, but she felt they often were in some ways more committed or more aware of commitment because of being constantly on call despite their reduced hours. Describing working with part-timers she observed:

> The people I know who work part time, they still, to this day, struggle with the same issues, the commitment issues, especially the more senior...who have tremendous responsibility.

Furthermore, some lawyers were aware that people could have multiple commitments and be committed to each one of them. John Dinsmore, a full-time supervisor who had worked three days a week for a year, forcefully stated his objections to the idea that part-time status indicated less interest in lawyering:

> Why can't people have multiple commitments? Why must law be a jealous lover? Who says that one must be exclusive to [one role] to be committed, invested, [or] loyal?

Alison Haft, a person deeply committed to social issues, arranged with the legal department of a large corporation to work three days a week so she could devote two days to working *pro bono* in the field of elder law. Unusually, her commitment to her profession went beyond commitment to a particular organizational setting.

Part-Time Lawyers Have to Prove Their Commitment

In various spheres of the law many part-time attorneys felt self-conscious about how their part-time status was interpreted. Some felt particularly scrutinized and strived to prove themselves. This included Judy Shine, a lawyer working for a government agency where part-time schedules are most formalized. Shine said she drives herself harder to prove she can do the work, and she was angry to be supervised more closely while working part time because her boss does not approve of her status.

Institutional Differences

Commitment issues vary in different types of legal organizations, although the equation that governs—time spent on the job equals commitment—may often transcend differences in the legal sectors. Firms do seem to act as "greedy institutions" in expecting (Coser and Coser, 1963) an enthusiastic and boundless time commitment. In government, a formal set of rules lays out the specific time boundaries of the workday. The norms in corporations lie somewhere between the two. The impact of part-time schedules on professional identity may depend on where the lawyer has been socialized, and the extent to which time norms define the professional role.[65]

Conflicting Expectations

Because lawyers move in and out of various sectors of the profession—for example, starting out in large firms and gravitating to government—they often face different expectations of commitment and bring with them attitudes that may clash with those of coworkers.

This is illustrated by Thelma Greene, who holds a job-sharing position in a corporate legal department. Her prior experience had been in a large corporate firm. Her job-sharing partner had worked in a government agency:

> I was working a lot harder than she was. She also felt I was working a lot harder too...[and] felt I was showing her up.... When I took time off I wanted her to cover; but when she took time off she didn't expect me to cover.... I just have a much more intense work ethic than Susan.... I have trouble leaving something undone on my desk at the end of the day. She has no trouble at all.

Perceptions of commitment varies with experience: Colleagues' perceptions of part-time lawyers' commitment often depend on whether they know their prior work history as full-time lawyers. As we noted in the discussion on mobility, colleagues who know them are more likely to define the part-timer as committed than those who encountered them only as part-timers.

Perception of commitment varies with visibility of part-time attorneys: Perception of commitment is linked to visibility. Part-timers typically do not work at the times of the day regarded as the greatest tests of commitment, after the regular 9-to-5 workday is ended. When part-timers do put in time after the normal workday, they draw benefit from it. Of course, most lawyers who choose a reduced schedule do so to be available for dinnertime with their children. One exception, however, was Laurie Babcock, a part-time corporation lawyer who recognized that she might be regarded as less committed than the full-timers and so arranged a schedule to come to the office later in the morning and stay late in the evening:

> There's a real ethic at the business to work all the time...so [because of my part-time status] they would think I'm less committed to them. [But] my preference for staying late in the evening helps, because they know they can call me at 6 and I'll be there.

Recognition of commitment: There were exceptions to the pattern of suspicion about the commitment of part-time attorneys. In several government offices, chiefs and deputy chiefs supervising part-time attorneys voiced appreciation of the commitment of the part-time lawyers working under them. Henry Baxter articulated the sentiments of a number of supervisors in an interview in which he described his experience with a part-timer:

> Julie sets an example—she doesn't encourage a model of lawyering which equates commitment with hours spent on the job.

> •   •   •

> [Generally] part-timers are not less committed. I've observed that they tend to be more concentrated and intense about their work than full-timers.

Gender Differences in Evaluations of Commitment

Perceptions of commitment are also colored by gender stereotypes. Clara Schumann was one of a number of part-time attorneys who felt that men's commitments were not questioned as much as women's:

> It is very sexist because men frequently have these other things that they do that take them away from work. They belong to this charity board, they do this volunteer work, but that is not viewed as a distraction from their commitment, but if a woman wants to work part-time...[that is].

Thus we see how part-time schedules are used as a proxy for commitment with consequences for attorneys' self-concept as professionals, for their working relationships with other attorneys, and for their mobility. Finally, time measures used as indicators for commitment further stigmatize part-time work.

CHAPTER 11

COLLEGIALITY

One of the most problematic aspects of part-time legal work is the limitation on relations with colleagues that results when lawyers work fewer hours and strive to make every one count. This translates into work at one's desk and little off-time during the workday, that is, few of the bits of time that full-time employees use for "schmoozing" (Schrank, 1978)—gossiping or "hanging out." The negative side of such efficient use of time is the shrinking of social ties on the job. It eliminates the nonwork aspects of work (Epstein, 1991), those activities that smooth work relationships or help one accomplish a goal, but that are not considered part of the job.[66]

Part-time associates in firms commonly reported they experience little or no collegiality. As Jean Fine, a seventh-year associate in a huge New York firm, commented:

> I come, I do my work, I leave. For a long time I didn't even take lunch. I would just do my work, eat at my desk.... My focus is to do my work and then to leave.

Yet casual talk and informal social relations created or reinforced over a lunch defined as social contribute to learning on the job. Individuals become acquainted with the politics of an organization or pick up references or ideas and get information about clients or the economy that might be useful to building business deals (Epstein, 1970, [1981] 1993). Women have long been concerned about being excluded from informal networks; not being asked to join colleagues for lunch or drinks may cut one off from important information about internal politics (Epstein *et al.*, 1995; Hall, 1946) or limit contacts that might be crucial for advancement.

Sometimes part-timers don't know what they are missing, and some of them dismiss the importance of these informal contacts. Others know they are missing a potentially important activity but feel that it is a sacrifice they must make and that they can make up for missed information by systematic gathering of information through other channels, such as research materials and newspaper accounts.

Furthermore, the pressure to produce high-quality work in a limited number of hours means that lawyers may not be able to participate in firm activities and social functions that might bring them into contact with partners and members of other departments who might provide them with contacts and clients.

On the other hand, part-time lawyers also are restricted by time limitations in offering others the benefit of their experience by talking informally with them. For example, they do not have much time to mentor less senior lawyers or to be part of training activities for incoming classes.

A concise account of the loss of collegiality came during an interview with Heather Lipton, a part-time government staff attorney:

> You're in the office fewer hours and...a lot of what we do here is collegial and sort of just legal schmoozing. And obviously if you're in three-fifths of the time, you [only] get three-fifths of that too.... That is a loss. It's a social loss, too.... There's a bunch of us who are...very, very good friends.... We've been here for a long time...a very definite social network that we depend on, and that [has decreased].... Being home...is isolating.

Some part-timers suffered pangs of disassociation from colleagues more than others. Phoebe Engelhardt, an eight-year part-time associate in a large firm, felt alienated:

> It's very hard.... I feel like an island in many ways. On many levels it's...miserable.

Gloria Stern reflected on her status as an independent contractor:

> I missed the structure. I missed having the colleagues, I missed belonging.... The downside of working in an entirely self-structured job was not belonging to something. Not having a specific organization and peers and identity. And I didn't realize how important it was to me. I liked feeling connected to an organization.

The limitations on collegiality differ, and some individuals are more competent at compensating for them than others. And, of course, some informal interactions are not productive and can be missed, though one never knows beforehand.

However, on balance, the norms of the legal workplace are such that as one moves toward coveted territory it is useful to engage in collegial activities, and those who must curtail them do so at some cost. According to an analysis in *Barron's,* a financial newspaper (1998), women have come up against a glass ceiling in the business and professional world partly because their family obligations undercut their bonding opportunities in the workplace (Epstein, 1997). Moreover, the psychic toll can be substantial; as part-timers experience distance from colleagues, their links to their organizations diminish, and they face boundary-less careers (Mirvis and Hall, 1994).

C H A P T E R   1   2

JUSTICE AND FAIRNESS

Equity is one of the major values of American society. Although not all cultural values are consistent, and some may even be contradictory,[67] the American value system stresses fairness and justice as a major theme and a matter of democratic principle. This theme is embedded in the values of the workplace (as it is in the rest of social life), where constant assessments are made of the fairness of the exchange of giving and receiving, of contribution and compensation.

Such assessments, which come down to the question of whether a person is believed to be delivering a fair day's work for a fair day's pay, are basic to the American worker. Although vast discrepancies exist in monetary rewards at the various levels of the occupational hierarchy (the sometimes huge contingency fees of malpractice attorneys and the high pay of top executives in industry are two examples),[68] strenuous attempts are usually made to justify differences in rewards in terms of the contributions people are said to make in performing work roles.[69] Of course, the notion of a *contribution,* when one considers such hard-to-quantify qualities as talent and "presence," may be socially constructed, and many explanations are merely justifications and do not reflect actual skills or accomplishments. However, it is important to note that justifications are required when the sense of equity has been disturbed.

Some categories of people are situated better than others to reap the benefit of generous assessments of their worth. It is the case that women's work has typically been regarded as less important than men's, and their average pay also is lower (England and Farkas, 1986; Epstein, 1970, 1988; Hacker, 1997). What individuals contribute and what they and others think they deserve is usually part of workplace culture and relevant to the question of what constitutes fairness in terms of hours at work.

Thus a code of "distributive justice" (Homans, 1961), based on a balance of costs, rewards, and investments (however calculated in a particular society or social group), functions to help people assess the extent to which fairness and reciprocity govern the social relations of work.[70]

It is not only fairness of remuneration, as we explained in our discussion of the economics of part-time work[71] but equality of industriousness that is assessed in the workplace. People who do not do their share—that is, who invest less than they should for the reward they receive according to a normative standard—are regarded negatively by coworkers and are sanctioned. In American society, terms such as goldbrickers and goof-offs indicate displeasure with some individuals' attempts to "get away" with doing less than their share of a task.

Gender Issues in the Evaluation of Fairness

Priorities in the culture specify the work and family roles that men and women are expected to perform. For men, family roles and work roles have not been in conflict, although this is changing today. For women it is another story.

One way this is expressed is in the notion of how much of life's rewards a woman (but not a man) ought to have. As women have moved into the workplace and acquired more highly evaluated public roles, the notion of the "superwoman" has been used as a pejorative. A vocabulary of sacrifice has been applied to women; they usually are regarded as paying a price for efforts to simultaneously meet family responsibilities and engage in the paid labor force. The idea of "having it all" is a judgment unfairly applied to women, not to men, condemning women who do manage both realms successfully. Our study of large law firms (Epstein *et al.*, 1995) found that generational differences were evident in assessments of what having it all meant. Senior women who had risen in their firms believed it was possible to combine multiple roles successfully, but a number of junior women thought there would have to be a cost—a cost they were not willing to pay—for efforts to attain both professional accomplishment and a good family life. Personal differences also guided individuals' assessments of how much cost was involved and what the "prices" were for involvement in family or work activity.

This evaluation system may operate to limit women's opportunities to manage careers and families and contribute to the "glass ceilings" that many report they encounter (Epstein *et al.,* 1995).

In the assessment of fairness of their own contributions, a number of the lawyers interviewed suggested they faced suspicions that they might not be pulling their weight. This was reported by Eileen Fawcett, a part-time partner in a small firm whose full-time partners saw her limited schedule as offering benefits beyond what her efforts warranted, giving her "a good deal."

Janet Ogilvy, a part-time attorney who had recently been laid off from a corporate job, could empathize with coworkers' suspicions about her contributions. She agreed her arrangement offered a better deal than those given the people she worked with:

> We were all very close-knit.... And I felt that the other full-time lawyers were supportive...but...a little bit resentful.... It wasn't expressed, but it was there. If I were sitting at my desk till 8 or 9 o'clock and [watching] somebody walking out every day and still getting paid well,...[it could cause resentment].

Often feelings of support and resentment were uneven or mixed among coworkers. Eleanor Strauss, a government attorney, reported, "Some see the unit as doing me a favor [and resent it]; others think it's great."

This resentfulness may also be interpreted as jealousy. Hillary Romer, a former part-time associate at a large firm, now working for a corporation, believed there was "a fair amount of jealousy" of her part-time arrangement among the male junior partners in her former firm. She observed that the men felt they must work full time because of economic pressures, and they regarded women's options and choices to work part time as a luxury.

> I think most of them were not happy. I would say almost all of them would have preferred to be doing something else. This is not what they thought would be happening to their lives when they became a partner in a major New York law firm.... Some would rather be judges or D.A.s, but the money is not enough for their lifestyle.... It is a compromise they've decided to make.

Some part-time attorneys reported feeling that people in their offices think they ought to be grateful for getting a special deal. Margaret Carroll, an attorney in a large corporation, said she thinks there is a tradeoff between receiving a part-time schedule and the sense of obligation that the lawyer is expected to feel:

> It has been sort of a "We'll do you this favor and let you do this, but you should be grateful and not complain."

Justifications for Part-Time Schedules

Motherhood is the primary reason given to seek and justify part-time work in the legal profession. It's one of the more powerful justifications for shedding full-time lawyering, but even this reason is subject to scrutiny for fairness. One woman attorney shared her thoughts about it:

> I think to the extent that you work part time and it makes other people around you work harder...they're less happy.... I think people are much more willing to give you slack about it if the reason you're running out and leaving work behind is if you have a one-year-old at home. I think it's less likely if you say, "Well, I just want more leisure time."...Child care is a reason people can understand. So I think that's why people give more women more slack than they would a guy.

One attorney noted that certain kinds of family demands were accepted as legitimate reasons for reducing her work hours, and others were not. Specific obligations, such as a child's school schedule (*e.g.*, coming home every day at 3 p.m.) were legitimate, but not more diffuse needs of children. Limited durations of part-time work are considered justified, say, until a child can enter nursery school at age three, but not open-ended arrangements.

Compensation

Ultimately, compensation is a system of evaluation. Thus it has both a tangible material impact and a symbolic meaning.

Part of the problem with determining fairness is the fact that the basis for all compensation in some legal spheres is variable. Part-timers working in firms with a lock-step compensation scheme may be better off because it is easy to calculate a percentage of some absolute amount of pay. However, in the firms where compensation is on a point system with separate assessments for billable hours, client development, and power of clients, it is far more difficult to assess. For example, one partner quoted in the chapter on economics stressed the problems of calculating pay:

> There is some resentment.... On what base do you measure three-fifths, and if you put in more time, do you get more hours or more money when no one else does?

Thus, corporate in-house and government lawyers often face less resentment from colleagues for working reduced schedules because their coworkers receive fixed salaries and often work a set number of hours. The part-time person receiving a percentage of full pay for working an equal percentage of full-time hours can be seen as being treated fairly.

But even in government, supervisors use compensation as a way to send a message to part-timers conveying approval or disapproval of their status. A number of part-time attorneys in one agency of the government complained about the attitude of a supervisor who denied bonuses to those working a reduced schedule.

This same mentality was reported by Stephanie Olney, a part-time government attorney, when she and her part-time colleagues figured out that over a series of years none had ever been rated a "4," the highest level of evaluation for performance and one that automatically produced a pay increase.

Part-Time Lawyers' Concern with Fairness

It was from part-time lawyers themselves that we heard the most concern about fairness and appearances of fairness. They, even more than their supervisors and colleagues, were vigorous about wanting to justify their position. They said they would rather be undercompensated than to have people think they were doing less than their share. Because the vast majority of them were women, the issue of fairness carried the weight of attitudes arising from general cultural views that women's commitments and contributions to the workplace take a back seat to their family commitments. As noted in the chapters on career mobility and commitment, women part-timers in law, like other women in the workplace, feel they must prove themselves.

This was especially true for part-time partners, some of whom worked what might be considered a full-time schedule but negotiated remuneration of 80 or 90 percent of their firms' partnership shares so they could take off a few days a month or work a regular (*e.g.,* 10 a.m. to 7 or 8 p.m.) workday. Although some pointed out that full-time colleagues might also take off time or work less than their most compulsive colleagues, they wanted to be especially "fair" because as women they felt they were scrutinized more than men.

Not all of the part-time lawyers who reported overproducing felt good about not receiving a proportionate share of compensation or of symbolic rewards. Some were bitter and believed they were unjustly treated. Yet, as we have showed, so many feel grateful to have the opportunity to work part-time and to keep their professional careers alive while childrearing that they feel there is a certain *quid pro quo* they must pay. Often the injustice they sense is weighed against this larger equation.

While questions of equity arise in each sector of the law we studied, how part-time work is judged differs in each area. Those who work in government agencies tend to be less concerned with the fairness of working reduced schedules, and this is explained in part by their rigid pay schedules, seniority-based promotions, and universalistic rules for eligibility. The tendency for government lawyers, and to a lesser extent many working in the legal departments of large corporations, to successfully resist encroachments of work on nonwork time also diminishes their resentment of colleagues who are working part-time. Yet the most important factor in obviating questions of fairness may be the taken-for-granted nature of part-time work in certain settings. Compared to the standards of large firms, the full-time schedules of government agencies and many in-house departments are already "reduced." Generally, attorneys in these settings, both part- and full-time, accept their lower pay as a reasonable cost for the positive aspects of working fewer hours. The most common form of resentment they reported was related to the ability of some to work part-time. For some full-time people, part-time work is the province of the well-to-do. A union official in one office said that he could not be concerned with part-timers' problems because none of the support staff could afford to work part time. The manager of a large division of a municipal agency asked that the interviewer's tape recorder be turned off when he enumerated the reasons why he thought part-time work was "a rich woman's problem."

Scholars and policy makers might ask how much alternative work models ought to cost in terms of remuneration and career mobility. Certainly the issue arouses constant discussion within the profession and in society at large.

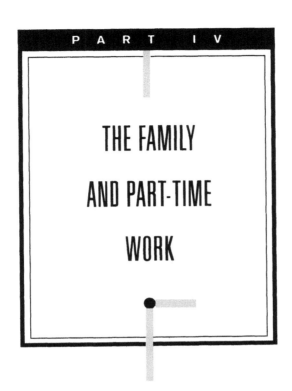

PART IV

THE FAMILY

AND PART-TIME

WORK

CHAPTER 13

PARENTS, CHILDREN, CHILD CARE, AND THE DIVISION OF LABOR IN THE FAMILY

The Role of Parents

Many of the issues that part-time professional work raises are linked to society's norms about the role of women and the care of children. Individual time and work priorities for parents, and especially working mothers, are shaped in part by questions of "family values," the sex division of labor, the rights of women, the needs of children, the "ideal family," and, of course, the psychologies of individual mothers and fathers. Although historically child care has been the responsibility of mothers, today fathers also are expected to share some of the obligations and to appreciate the attendant satisfactions of child care. But it continues to be defined as a woman's issue, and, as we have seen, it has generated pressures to institutionalize part-time work in the legal profession.

In the post–World War II era and for a time thereafter (Skolnick, 1991) the model of a stay-at-home, nonwage-earning mother caring for children represented an ideal in American society. Although women were actually moving into the workforce in ever-increasing numbers, the advent of the woman's movement in the late 1960s imbued women's presence in the labor force with a legitimacy that went beyond the economic pressures driving them there. At the same time, restrictions on their participation in high-prestige professions were seriously curbed through Title VII of the Civil Rights Act of 1964 and a series of landmark court cases.[72] In the years that followed, women flocked to the legal profession (Epstein, [1981] 1993) as they did to medicine and other spheres from which they had been excluded in the past. Indeed, mothers all over America have gone back to work after the birth of their children in numbers that have increased sharply in recent years. Fifty-five percent of new mothers returned to the workforce in 1995 within 12 months of giving birth, compared with 31 percent in 1976 when the Bureau of Labor Statistics started to track these figures (Fiore, 1997). Seventy-seven percent of college-educated women ages 30 to 44 juggle work and child rearing.

Of course, this trend conflicts with today's norms of motherhood, which specify standards for "intensive mothering" that have become ever more demanding (Coser and Coser, 1974; Hays, 1996). Standards for "quality time" with children have also escalated the numbers of hours each week parents are supposed to devote to involvement in their children's education, psychological development, and leisure-time activities (Hays, 1996).

At the same time, child care—private and public day-care centers, all-day nurseries, agencies that supply nannies and baby-sitters for those who can afford private solutions—all cater to the child-care needs of working parents.[73] However, there is not enough high-quality child care generally available to meet demand, and there are also cultural perspectives that make the use of surrogates (except for family members) problematic.

The backlash against working mothers has been reflected in a stream of books (Hewlett, 1986; Mack, 1997; Whitehead, 1997), newspaper and magazine articles, and television news stories. From the mainstream press to the publications of right-wing organizations and "foundations," features are published constantly decrying the use of surrogate care. Working women are directly or indirectly chastised for selfishness in articles such as "Day Careless" (Gallagher, 1998) in *National Review;* "Day Care: The Thalidomide of the 1980s"[74] and "Working Moms, Failing Children,"[75] in publications of the Rockford Institute; and cover stories in national newsmagazines such as "The Myth of Quality Time: How We're Cheating Our Children" in *Newsweek* and "The Lies Parents Tell About Work, Kids, Money, Day Care and Ambition" in *U.S. News and World Report.* News coverage focuses on stories about inadequate, inappropriate, and even lethal caregivers (Barnett and Rivers, 1997). Sociologist Arlie Hochschild's (1997) claim that Americans prefer working to dealing with the stresses of parenting received much media attention, including a cover story in the *New York Times Magazine,* and evoked a lively public response faulting American women for their selfishness in preferring the workplace to the home. And the case of Louise Woodward, an English *au pair* worker acquitted in the death of an infant in her care in a Boston suburb, generated an avalanche of hate mail to the mother, a part-time physician, faulting her for not caring for her child herself.

The hostility and indifference expressed by the media to their child-care needs and the arrangements they make fuels guilt in working mothers and reinforces conventional negative attitudes about the advisability of full-time mothers' care for children (Faludi, 1991).

Women have written about the continuing conflict between their roles, seeing it as a war between their "selves." For example, in a book explaining her retreat from a high-powered publishing position to become a more attentive mother, Elizabeth Perle McKenna (1997:85) wrote:

> Every morning the bell would ring and out would come these two identities, sparring with one another, fighting for the minutes on the clock and for my attention.

Research that shows positive effects on the family well-being of dual-career couples (Barnett and Rivers, 1997; Parcel and Menanghan, 1994) does not evoke the same kind of media attention that bad experiences evoke, and virtually no media coverage focuses on the benefits to children of surrogate care or the successful management of roles by worker-mothers.

Thus, cultural contradictions of mothering have deepened rather than resolved concerns about the balancing of work and family obligations (Hays, 1996).

Though all the mothers among the lawyers interviewed for this study rely on at least part-time surrogate care, they are wary about delegating child care and seek to minimize it. Although even full-time working mothers express some ambivalence about assigning part of their mothering role to another person, part-timers have chosen reduced work schedules as a way to express their preferences and reduce their guilt, and, of course, to reduce role strain (Goode, 1960; Merton, 1957). A refrain common in many of the interviews with part-time lawyers was expressed by an associate at a large firm: "No one, no one, not a nanny, not a day-care center, will show my children as much love, and be able to care for my children the way that I can." Josh Levanthal, a supervising attorney in a government agency, worked part time to share in care for his children, as did his wife, Robin, another government attorney. Josh told us he agreed with his wife in thinking "a nonparent would not take the same sort of care that a parent would." Similarly, Sara Wright, an associate in a medium-size law firm whose office shelves were filled with photographs of her two toddlers, expressed concern that her children "have [my] moral values and not the babysitter's" and said this motivated her to take a part-time schedule.

Some of the lawyers interviewed expressed distrust of surrogates. Marina Goff, who cut back her work schedule after moving to a distant suburb so she could spend more time with her two-year-old son and five-year-old daughter, spoke of the "horror stories you hear, even from friends." Several other lawyers also spoke of the "absolute nightmare to find people who can watch your children." Fueled by newspaper accounts of horrible behavior by nannies,[76] two of the attorneys interviewed admitted secretly videotaping their in-home child-care providers. Both were pleasantly relieved to discover that their children had exemplary care.

Of course, this cultural climate has had an effect on attitudes about how much commitment working mothers ought to have to their careers, and how much to the family. These cultural attitudes persuade many women to work less and a few to leave the workplace altogether for the sake of "motherhood," although discontent about the nature of their work may also contribute to retreat from career paths.

McKenna's (1997) study of women who decide to leave work found that when she scratched the surface, "women admitted that, yes, they wanted more flexibility and time for their children, but if they had been happier in their work, they would have figured it out somehow" (164). She pointed to the case of Alicia Daymans, who declared in an early part of an interview that she decided to leave the high-profile magazine she worked for because she wanted to spend more time with her daughter, but revealed later that the "real" reasons were the moral and philosophical differences she had with the publication's owners. Certainly, spending time with her preadolescent daughter was a big concern, but she admitted that this alone would not have prompted her to leave.

Certainly, many women feel it is appropriate to work full time and use child-care surrogates, and do. We interviewed scores of women attorneys in our study of lawyers in large corporate law firms (Epstein *et al,* 1995) who said they were comfortable with the balance of work and family in their lives and had worked with responsible and loving child-care surrogates who served their families well. This supported David Chambers's (1989) striking findings that women graduates of the Michigan Law School who were mothers showed the highest amount of contentment when compared with childless women (married and single) and with men. Although many of them worked part-time for some period after law school, many either consistently worked full-time or swiftly returned to full-time work after a brief leave. Consistent with our findings, women with children in Chambers's sample made more accommodations to career than men. Most for some period since law school ceased working outside the home or shifted to part-time work. A quarter of the mothers worked part-time or took leaves for periods totaling at least 18 months. But even women who do not feel guilty about sharing themselves with career and family must interact with others who question their behavior and punish them.

Several lawyer mothers complained that some "stay-at-home" mothers refused to make playdates with their children, if the nanny brought the child to their home. As a result many women are exposed to multiple and often contradictory messages.[77] The women and the few men who choose part-time work, or the law jobs with "regular hours" considered less than the large-firm norm, are those who hope to reconcile the obligations and satisfactions of both spheres using an alternative equation. Part-timers particularly subscribe to the hands-on parenting norms popular today and are members of socioemotional communities that foster them. Pressures from spouses, children, coworkers, extended family members, and social acquaintances all affect what they say, believe, and do about balancing familial duties and professional calling.

It appears that the families of the lawyers who use part-time work in law firms to resolve the conflicts of work and child care are not so different structurally than the families of their full-time lawyer colleagues (Epstein *et al.*, 1995). They are about the same size and are headed by spouses who work in similar occupations, for example.

More than 80 percent (62 out of 75) of the lawyers in this study who work or have worked part time chose to do so for child-care reasons. They are mothers (with two exceptions) whose children ranged in age from infancy to 13 years old. Several mothers chose to work reduced hours from the time that they returned to work from maternity leave; others chose it as their children moved beyond infancy, and still others after the birth of a second child. About 40 percent either have returned or plan to return to full-time employment as their children mature (22 of 57), and 12 percent (7) are unsure of their plans. Almost half (28 lawyers) have no present intention of resuming full-time work. Additionally, most lawyers responding to a survey sent out by the Part-Time Network of the Association of the Bar of the City of New York (the LAWWS Network) (Schwab, 1994)—a group promoting part-time options in the legal profession—answered that they did not wish to return to full-time work in the future. A subset of our sample has migrated back and forth between full-time and part-time status as their families have increased in size, grown older, or been affected by other work or family pressures.

Decisions to Work Part-Time for the "Joys of Motherhood"

Just as these lawyers reported that their decisions to have children were worked out strategically in terms of their careers, more than half of the women part-timers in this study reported that when they were pregnant they were fairly certain that they would not return to work full-time after giving birth. Yet, of these, many told us that for strategic purposes, they behaved at work "as if" they were unsure about their postpartum plans. They did not want to reveal their intentions to work part-time prior to taking maternity leave because they did not want to lose quality work before they took leave, and they also believed they could negotiate a more favorable reduced-hours arrangement later. For most of the women in the study the decision to work part time was cushioned because they are wives of prosperous men. Thus, they were financially free to act on their feelings that it was necessary to spend more time at home.

Psychological reactions to motherhood compelled a number of lawyers interviewed to choose part-time work. Some reported their decisions to take extended periods of maternity leave or return on a part-time basis were spontaneous and emotionally unpredictable. As Patricia Clarke, a senior associate in a large Wall Street firm, described it:

> I fell madly in love with my son.... I just started to feel that I wouldn't be able to leave him every day and feel like someone else was raising my child. I didn't love my job enough to justify that.... It wasn't a trade-off worth making.

Cheryl Meany, a government attorney who left a position at a medium-size firm because she could not reduce her work schedule from four to three days a week, was agitated when she remarked, "I just felt desperate to be with my child." She admitted to being more traditional than other lawyers and wishing to stay home to take care of her two preschool-age daughters, but she was not alone in feeling "desperate."

Several mothers noted that the urge to work part time was fueled by jealous competition with their care providers. Gloria Mann, another government attorney, declared that she needed to spend "every waking hour" with her new son because:

> Being a mother to him... I felt like every minute,... every weekend I would be there for him to know that I was his mother, [not the]... baby-sitter.

Another mother admitted that she was heartbroken to find a local store clerk mistake her son's *au pair* for her.

Cultural lore stresses the value of witnessing a child's first steps or first words. The importance of these moments was internalized by many of the women (but was not reported by fathers in the same way). In her interview, Betty Forten, a full-time attorney, wept softly as she described her feelings at missing her son's first successful attempt at walking, a major regret of the women who worked full time. In her study of child-care providers, *Other People's Children* (1995), the sociologist Julia Wrigley found that nannies know the cultural importance of such infant milestones and that many refrain from telling parents when their children utter their first words or take their first steps, so that the mother or father will "discover" these achievements themselves.

The importance of witnessing and participating in the later development of a child was the rationale for their choice as Barbara Friedl, an eighth-year associate in a large, expanding firm, explained:

> I discovered that the more verbal they get, the more incredibly engaging they are. And the more my presence makes a difference to them. And right now, for a five-year-old... there is no one in the universe like me.... Her baby-sitter is wonderful and she adores her... but there is something absolutely extraordinary about having Mommy pick her up from school.

Profile of Families and Child-Care Arrangements

What do families in which the part-time lawyering choice is made look like? To draw this portrait we rely only on the 84 lawyers in the sample who returned questionnaires asking about their families and other socioeconomic data. The composition of their families and the child-care provisions they have made are as follows:

Marital status: Part-time lawyers typically are married. There is one single mother among the lawyers who answered the questionnaire and one childless single attorney whose part-time arrangement was negotiated to provide time to pursue other interests.

Employment of spouse: Most of the part-time lawyers' spouses were employed in law, finance, and other professional work (see Table 13.0; Appendix C). It seems evident that lawyers who choose to work part time rely on the income of a full-time working spouse. In general, women in households with higher levels of other income, either higher spousal earnings or larger amount of non-earned household income, are more likely to work part time than other women (Blank, 1990).

Size of family: The lawyers in this study have small families (see Table 13.1; Appendix C), with a norm of two children, like other professional families. About half (48 of 84) have two children. Eight of the lawyers in the sample had more than two children, and eight had none (although these were young and anticipated having children). Many of the women had not had children until they were past the age of 30.

Child-care arrangements: These lawyers use a wide variety of child-care arrangements[78] (see Table 13.2; Appendix C). They rely on relatives, daily or live-in nannies, or day care. Almost one-half (32 of 69) of those for whom we have data use live-in or live-out full-time (i.e., full-week) care providers. Twenty-two families employ part-time providers as their primary child care, and the remaining 15 use baby-sitters, relatives, or day care.

A couple's resources of course affect the child-care arrangements they make. The high-income lawyers tend to use the most child care. Among families with high incomes, full-time or live-in nannies predominate (see Table 13.3; Appendix C). Of the 29 families for whom we have both income and employment sector data, 25 with family incomes of more than $150,000 have live-in nannies. Twenty-two of those lawyers are employed by large private law firms. A number of lawyers in large firms employ housekeepers as well as nannies, and some also have additional staff to take care of their country homes. Nannies were also employed by six lawyers who worked in the legal departments of corporations, by one self-employed lawyer, and by one government agency lawyer. About half (10 of the 22) of those who use part-time care providers work for government agencies, and four of the five using day care work in government agencies.

The nature of the attorneys' work is related closely to their incomes and thus is a determining factor in the type of child care they choose (see Table 13.4). The nature of the work may be a consideration in another way as well. Not only do attorneys in large firms and in corporate settings have the money to hire a nanny, but the demands on their time for schedule flexibility and the "on-call" nature of their work are believed to require it. Such flexibility typically cannot be put together at the last minute on an *ad hoc* basis. A few husbands have schedules that are predictable or flexible enough to permit them to pick up their children after school or day care or to relieve a sitter at the end of the day, and a small number of these part-time lawyers rely on them or on members of their extended families to do so. The more typical scenario, however, is that the husband's schedule is deemed to be more demanding than that of his wife, and she is expected to fill in the gaps in child care.

Seventeen sets of attorney couples were among the 32 families who employ full-time child-care providers. Five attorneys with full-time help have spouses who work in the financial sector. The lawyers whose spouses are academic professionals do not employ full-time or live-in nannies. But this lack of full-time coverage may be a reflection of the relatively greater flexibility of both spouses' work schedules rather than lower income.

Many lawyers rely on extraordinary flexibility and commitment from their child-care providers.[79] Patricia Borden, a government staff attorney who works three days a week, is married to another attorney. She requires an at-home child-care provider who can stretch her own workday to care for her two children. Day-care centers available to her have strict time limits and are not "flexible the way a human can be." She remarked,

I have…a tremendously flexible arrangement, both the after-school for him [her older son], and a sitter [for her toddler] for as long as I need her. She's tremendously flexible. If she has some appointment, she'll clear it with me. And then I'll know that I absolutely have to be home by then. Otherwise it's easy to sort of bleed into 7 o'clock without trying hard. So my days are generally sort of 9:30 to 7.

"Family-Friendly" Work Settings

Some places of legal employment are more desirable than others because of their "family-friendly" atmosphere. A Westchester, New York, manufacturing concern at which we interviewed part-time attorneys has such a reputation. There, breaking away from work to attend a child's soccer game or ballet recital is considered necessary. In this setting, women with small children often are given work assignments with little or no travel. But official organizational friendliness may not solve the interpersonal problems that develop because of different parental statuses of employees. For instance, questions of fairness were raised by two childless women attorneys when they were asked to increase their work travel so that a woman attorney with children could be freed from travel obligations. When one of them balked she was queried by her supervising attorney, "What's the matter? You don't have any kids."

One government agency has a reputation for being a good place for parents to work because of its flexibility toward part-time commitments and a staff with a large percentage of parents with young children. Patricia Brooke, who moved from a lucrative position at a midsize firm, spelled out why she sought employment there:

It was very interesting work, a three-day-a-week schedule…and mostly the head of this department was very supportive of part-time people and did not consider them to be second-class citizens. At my previous firm, while I was part time…. I was certainly a second-class citizen.

Negotiating Part-Time Status with a Spouse

Decisions about childbearing, time off, and part-time work were pondered and made by these lawyers within a broad context that incorporated economics, norms of professional commitment, and ideas about gender roles. The decision about which spouse will work part time is generally made against three criteria: a "rational" economic assessment, the couple's response to traditional sex roles, and their agreed-upon ideology. All of these criteria may be seen as ide-

ological concepts that are intertwined and susceptible to challenge and negotiation.

There are economic repercussions on the family when a spouse cuts back
work time and income, but because of the income differentials in the various
sectors of the profession the impact on family lifestyle may vary. Usually, when
a spouse cuts back on work time, family income falls precipitously. Virtually all
families decide jointly whether to reduce paid labor from two full-time jobs,
and most couples negotiate over how much their work schedules can be
reduced and what child-care arrangements can be made. Many husbands ini-
tially were reluctant to accept their wives' working a reduced schedule, but
others saw this as the wife's decision. Patricia Brooke said her husband, Tom,
was skeptical about her working part time, for financial and professional reasons. "He was...thinking, 'Gee, we're now gonna be poor,'" she said. Tom is
also a lawyer and has doubts about the seriousness and legitimacy of part-time
lawyering.

> The fact that we're both lawyers in many ways makes the relationship difficult,
> because he has...standards, and he doesn't think of part-time lawyers as...seri-
> ous.... He would never admit any of this, but I think his reluctance about part-
> time [makes him see] me as less legitimate as a lawyer because I'm only working
> three days.

The decision about which spouse will work full-time is rarely couched
today in the language of traditional roles, but is usually justified in terms of
maximizing income over a long time period. Yet studies show that it is common for men to regard themselves as the "breadwinner" no matter how much
income a wife brings into the family (Potuchek, 1997). Indeed, we heard from
a male government attorney that many of his colleagues had come to the
agency because of idealistic motivations to "help people," but found their
salaries could not support growing families, home mortgages, and wives who
felt they should cut back in their own careers. Moving to legal work that was
more lucrative was, therefore, the "daddy track." Thus we see many decisions
are interactive with people's views of appropriate roles and future needs.
Couples weigh effort versus return; sacrifices are calculated against potential
gains. Many husbands have incomes sufficient to forgo their wives' contributions. When the men are in independent professional practices or are small-
business owners, couples usually decide it is more important to invest in his
career than hers. Finally, families often use the language of economic rational-
ization when deciding which spouse should work part time. Karyn Post works
four days a week as a senior associate in the corporate department of a prestigious midtown New York firm. She was hired on a part-time basis from a firm
where she also had worked a reduced schedule. She has no plans to return to

a full-time schedule and does not need to because her husband does very well working in the financial sector. She describes the process through which she and her husband agreed that she should work a reduced schedule:

> We decided that the financial rewards of partnership versus the hours that I would have to work to accomplish that were not worth it, and that it was better for me to go part-time and take on a bigger role at home.... I'm happy I was able to do that because I'd rather be at home and be with the kids. It was better to invest more in his career.

As we have seen, women report that they, together with their husbands, often make the decision to work part-time because they accept the idea that men will ultimately make more money than women. This is based on common knowledge that in general, women workers make less money for equal or similar work. Although this is not really the case for *professional* women who work in the same spheres as men and put in the same amount of time, couples still regard it as logical to invest in the husband's career.

Of course, powerful norms setting appropriate gender roles form a backdrop to all of these decisions even when the stated rationales are economic.

But sometimes, traditional sex-role assignments are a clearly stated factor in such decisions. Fiona Scott, a federal attorney, remarked that she was "more maternalistic than [her] husband was paternalistic." Others reported their husbands were uninterested in child rearing. Carrie Little, an associate at a large firm, explained that her husband did not consider reducing his work schedule because "he didn't really want to stay home and take charge.... He's more of a male." The traditional gender roles are not necessarily seen as "natural," but many regard them as inevitable. Jeannette Warren, a part-time partner at a prestigious firm, left her first job in the public interest sector in the early 1970s because it did not permit her to take a reduced schedule. She had the major responsibility for child care, a responsibility she desired. As she outlined her thinking:

> Women have...family responsibilities...that men just don't have.... My husband could do anything that I would do with my girls, but there were times when they just wanted me; and the other side of it is... maternal instinct,... I wanted to take them to the doctor; I didn't want him to take them to the doctor.... Women genetically or instinctively [are different].

Several mothers attributed their husbands' relative disinterest in child care to societal norms. "Of course, I wish my husband were more involved, but he's not. Society just doesn't value that for men, and he's just not that different from other men."

As the husband of a part-time lawyer described it, many attitudes come from the general society about the propriety of men and women taking on certain work and family roles. Philip Smith, an associate in a large firm, talked to us about having considered going part-time himself. He and his wife discussed it "jokingly...with an edge of seriousness." Sex roles played a major part in his thinking:

> You're brought up and programmed to think you're supposed to be and do [certain things].... And I guess you're brought up to think that well, if someone works part-time, it's going to be the wife. That's just how it is. And how shocking it would be if it was any other way.

Even if the subject is broached, the mechanisms that persuade people to conform to society's norms are sometimes right on the surface. Sharon Winick, a seventh-year associate in a large firm, recounted a discussion with her husband:

> Some of the issues [my husband and I discussed] were: Is it easy for a man to work part time? Is the stigma greater on a man? Can he ever redeem himself if he does that? Is it even possible to do that? He didn't experience the pull to want to be home. He experienced it as wanting to support me.

A part-time attorney whose husband is a lawyer who works at home confronted the cultural view of her husband's decision: "Real men do not work at home."

Ideological Renegades

When men chose to work part-time they explained it in ways that seemed a conscious attempt to subvert social norms and to offer themselves as alternative examples. They tended to have a political commitment to a gender-free ideology and a commitment to raising their children with maximum parental involvement. Robert Malcolm worked part-time for two years beginning four months after his first child was born. His father had played a very traditional role as a parent, which made him seek a different role. "I don't understand why men would want it to be any other way in...their relationships with their kids," he said. Equality of responsibility in child rearing is also a political issue, as he described it:

> In terms of household responsibilities...it's sort of a political issue. I come from the left side of the spectrum, and I'm a fairly strong feminist, and I think it's the proper way to live your life.

• • •

It was important to us that the kids viewed us equally. It was important to us that they didn't view the stereotyped roles for men and women in the household, ... that the kids basically had parents home with them for most of the time.

His wife, Leila, has worked three days a week in a municipal agency for two years and will continue to do so for the foreseeable future; she supports his decision. She feels that the reward for this political commitment was the way in which their son was socialized. "My son was totally equally bonded to both parents. He didn't have one primary over the other," she said. Their larger political commitment to set themselves as an example was important in this decision:

We did it [worked part time] for ourselves, but we were really happy [to] set an example.... When [only] a few men do it...you'll continue to have a situation where women rank behind men. Women will always be doing other things at home, and men will keep advancing their careers. So we both thought that the best thing would be if [we] share child-care responsibility.

In both cases where men worked reduced schedules to be with their children they became dissatisfied, feeling they were missing out on their careers and failing to enjoy their parenting roles. Both male lawyers returned to full-time work, leaving their wives to work part time. One of the men returned to a full-time schedule because he missed the supervisory role that is denied in his department to part-timers; the other, because of a trial that required his full-time participation. As we found in our study of large corporate firms (Epstein *et al.,* 1995), most men find that attempts to adjust their work schedules to accommodate family needs meet extreme resistance from employers, and the costs they face are felt to be too high to pay (Rhode, 1997). It is simply easier for their wives to find accommodation in the workplace.

Furthermore, sometimes knowingly and sometimes quite unconsciously, many women place constraints on their husbands' interest in reducing their workloads and spending more time with their children. Some who have tried it find also that women in the community resist their attempts to participate in parenting that goes beyond the traditional father's role as a soccer or baseball coach. John Spiegel, a government attorney whose wife works for the same agency two days a week on site, two days at home, told us it was clear that his wife "had more of a need" to be with the children. He felt also that if he spent more time at home he would be more isolated because he didn't think he'd be included in the activities arranged by mothers. Several mothers were candid about not encouraging their husbands to reduce their work time, saying they wished to be in charge at home. With a husband whose commitment to child care might be the envy of many working mothers, Sara Atkins found herself feeling quite ambivalent. A woman with two post-graduate degrees from elite schools, she left a full-time, high-demand position in a firm because of health problems and a desire to mother her two children. She intimated that her husband's active involvement with the children threatened her role as "primary parent," and she felt somewhat competitive with him. Her work choice effectively undercut her husband's plan to share the parenting role in an equitable way.

Professional Ideology

Many factors influence an attorney's choice of part-time work. One of the issues for women in law is the conflict between motherhood and the ideology of professionalism. As noted earlier, many of the profession's leaders regard law as a "calling."[80] It is this sense of vocation that partly differentiates a profession from a craft and sets it above other occupations.

Mothers who choose part-time work must adjust to the perception that they are compromising their calling. Of course, many young lawyers, men and women alike, no longer accept this definition of a professional. (It was only among lawyers in government service that we found a sense of mission to accomplish socially useful objectives. Yet even there the attractions of law were its autonomy, variety of work, and potential for a high income, rather than a grandiose ideal.) Margaret Segrest, a recently laid-off counsel in a multinational corporation's legal department with two boys and an attorney husband, expressed a sentiment that was not uncommon:

> I enjoy practicing law...I want to keep my foot in for economic reasons.... I like getting dressed and coming to work, and I like thinking, and I did invest a lot in going to law school.

What distinguishes a professional from a nonprofessional, in her view, is the professional's commitment to task without regard to other constraints. In contrast to a job in which one just does the required work within a given time period, a professional is supposed to be dedicated to producing the best she can and to provide service at its highest level.

In balancing physical, emotional, and time demands between lawyering and mothering, the allocation of energies required for mothering becomes less problematic for many part-time attorneys when the practice of law is reduced to "work, money, and prestige," as a lawyer sharing a job put it. The choice between children and career, as one woman expressed it, is a "no-brainer." Or as another joked, "There's a saying that on our deathbed nobody ever says, 'Gee, I wish I'd spent more time at work.'"

The Household Division of Labor:
Consequences of Part-Time Work

As Seron (1996) points out, the professions in general and the legal profession in particular depend on a gendered division of labor in the home. Totally dedicated male lawyers depend on their wives to handle household duties whether they stay at home or work full time or part time. As in dual-career families studied by Arlie Hochschild (1989), even an "equal" division of household labor tended to be a division of tasks inside and outside the house with unequal results. Several women reported that their husbands shared equally in household tasks, but when those cases are examined the division of labor follows traditional patterns, with men responsible for being "handy," *i.e.,* caring for the car and yard, making repairs, and filling in with some cooking or household chores. Women will more typically manage recurring household finances, do laundry and household chores, and be responsible for all child-care duties. Moreover, women in this study had a common complaint: Their husbands "just don't notice." Even those men who accepted responsibility for housework and child care had to be supervised, in their wives' view. By doing chores that fit within the definition of being handy or neglecting details of housework, men "do gender," in the words of the sociologists Candace West and Don Zimmerman (1987). The ways in which they divide up household tasks and how they do them allow men to reaffirm their gendered identities. Elsie Marshak works as a part-time associate 35 hours a week, or 70 percent of a 50-hour full-time position, at a large firm in midtown Manhattan. With three daughters ranging in age from two to nine, she and her husband, an executive in the electronics industry, employ a full-time nanny. As she described the division of labor in her household:

> It's hard to pinpoint specific jobs. He helps clean up dinner, he helps prepare dinner sometimes. He helps me with the children in the evening. We have our own division that's hard to put into a two-sentence summary. He does everything outside the house. I do everything inside the house. Like, all the bill paying, the party arrangements, vacations, social planning...doctor's appointments, kids. I do everything for the kids, clothing, parties, RSVPs, I mean I delegate some of that to the nanny but, basically, it's my responsibility. Basically, I run my house. I delegate things to him.

Another attorney describes herself as the "hunter-gatherer of the family who does all the shopping, cooking, and arranging of things" while her husband is the handyman. By taking on the lion's share of household duties, women allow their spouses to pursue their careers or develop businesses. Some women work part-time so that they can devote more time to household chores in addition to child-rearing responsibilities. By doing these things on weekdays they free weekends for family social activities.

Not all of the women lawyers in our sample embraced or even fully accepted their role in the gendered division of labor in the household. Charlotte Henry, a government attorney, was deeply resentful that when she went part-time her husband expected her to take on more traditional wifely domestic responsibilities such as cooking, cleaning, and shopping.[81] This was not what she had in mind when she reduced her work schedule. In her view, her husband imposed an old framework—assuming that she would spend her time away from work as his mother did, at household tasks. But Ms. Henry chose to go to the gym and engage in other personal interests when child-care responsibilities did not interfere. "Time for oneself" was an issue for many women.

Men's involvement with their children ranged from the father who worked part-time so that he could be a primary caregiver to those who worked long hours and spent little time with their offspring. Most women think that their husbands spend relatively more time and give more attention to their children than men in previous generations, but they are also aware that the traditional role structure has not changed radically. Caren Petrie, a senior associate at a large firm, said of her husband:

> Actually, he's good. In fact, if I tell him, he'll do [household chores]. I wish some-times he'd do things without my telling me. He's actually very good with the kids. He'll spend a lot more time than my father did with the kids. And, I think, than what his father did. But he has the *good* time with the kids. He doesn't do the grunt work, which I take care of. All the schools and the insurance stuff.

Cheryl Mobry, who works in a municipal legal department, told how her hus-band once wanted to work a reduced schedule but changed his mind and instead works long hours. "He loves the kids, and I think he'd certainly like to get home earlier.... But when he has a day by himself with the kids, he's not all excited about it, which I am." She saw an irony in this situation: Middle- and upper-middle-class women can add to their family income, but it has not significantly changed traditional roles. She expanded on this:

> It was actually a joint decision that it made more sense for us for him to work hard, for me to take more of a responsibility at home—I take care of everything; he does very little. And he is spoiled. I think that because of women's lib the men have made out very well, because the women bring in money, but still do what their mothers did, and the husbands, it takes a lot to get them to move.

Part-Time Work as a Solution for Role Strain and Role Inequities

Faced with cross-pressures to meet the norms of intensive mothering, the problems of surrogate child care, the curtailing of professional identity, and the continued strength of traditional gender roles in the family, what keeps women lawyers, who usually can afford to, from leaving the paid work force altogether?

Two issues predominate: the fatigue and isolation of parenting, and the attempt to maintain power in marital relationships.

Most of the women lawyers interviewed saw their work as a needed respite from domestic responsibilities. Elsie Marshak, the associate described earlier as working 35 hours a week in a large firm, considers work a condition for sanity: "I need to work. I would go crazy staying at home full time. But I was also going to go crazy doing everything at once." Using similar language, Laurie Potempkin, another part-time associate, asserted, "I think that I would go crazy staying at home. I need some structure to my life. I need the intellectual stimulation. And kids are great. But they're very demanding; it's very physically demanding and not as intellectually so in the early years." She went on to describe mothering as lonely and isolating:

> When I was on maternity leave, I found it lonely. There wasn't the camaraderie of working with people, the interaction with colleagues; you just sit with other mothers. But I guess maybe I didn't click with the other mothers. They were just always talking about kids and play days and stuff.

The gendered division of labor exists and persists because of differences in power between men and women. Some women respond to this imbalance by asserting their need for independence. Part-time work allows them to keep some control over their financial resources, social networks, and professional identities. In large part, they are defending a space with both real and symbolic territories. Their social networks and professional identities are reminders that they are more than mothers. Although, with a few notable exceptions, women attorneys do not earn enough in part-time positions to maintain their standard of living, their earnings are considerable compared to what they would earn in other occupations. Further, an independent income offers the possibility of autonomy; its absence means dependence.[82] In negotiating conflicting norms, they often use their mothers' experience as a guide, stressing their continued employment as a safety net. Elsie Marshak reflected:

> My parents...had a rocky marriage for 30 years, and my mother always pushed me to be financially independent.... I'm not truly independent. Our lives are so

intertwined with kids, but [it's important] knowing that, if I want independence, I can have it.

Though Deborah Seinfield, in her 40s, removed herself from the partnership track, staying in the labor force as a part-time associate gives her a sense of independence:

> I never thought I'd be able to depend on somebody else…for money…. One of the things that's always kept me from quitting, other than the fact that my husband says, "No," was I couldn't imagine asking him for money, for an allowance.

Neither of these attorneys believe their incomes make them self-sufficient, but they are grounds for claiming at least symbolic autonomy.

The integration of work roles and family roles is negotiated by husbands and wives on the basis of their philosophies, traditions, and practical concerns. Financial pressures, the number of children and their ages, and access to good child-care providers are all important factors, but all are weighed and interpreted within frameworks that mark the pair's private worlds and reflect the larger society.

PART V

TECHNOLOGY

CHAPTER 14

TECHNOLOGY AND PART-TIME LAWYERING

The Positive and Negative Functions of Technology

As their documents and messages zoom across the globe in a moment through e-mail, airline phones, faxes, and computer transfers, lawyers find that new technologies have paradoxical consequences for their lives. Technology allows some lawyers to work part-time and escape the worst of this intensified work cycle. Yet, because technology expedites work, part-timers can accomplish appreciable amounts of work on their restricted schedules.

Using the new communications technologies—most of them common only in the past 15 years or less—lawyers and clients now have easier access to each other and, as we have seen, their relationships have been affected by the shortened turnaround time that technology makes possible (Jacobs and Gerson 1997). "Socially expected durations" (Merton, 1984) have been compressed with respect to lawyers' availability to their clients and clients' expectations for completion of work and its delivery. The new technologies engender rising expectations that work can be completed in less time, and lawyers must live with increasing pressures to get work done quickly and efficiently. Cecilia McCoy, an associate at a midsize boutique law firm, described a coworker in Manhattan:

> [She]...is sort of a permanent attorney—not a partner, not an associate—who has kids, five and seven. She's made a superhuman effort to accommodate both [work and home]. She was the first person to have a cellular phone; she's the first person to have a fax at home. She's the first person to have the system wired at home.

As McCoy suggests, technology provides lawyers with tools to be available for clients from just about any location and at any time; thus, the "virtual office" permits one to work from home, car, or even a vacation cabin in the Rockies. The new technologies both ease and undermine the juggling act required of part-time arrangements in a highly demanding profession like law.

Technology in the Professional Workplace

The introduction of computers, cellular phones, faxes, and e-mail systems must be examined in the social, cultural, and historical context of each arena of work. These technologies have altered interpersonal relationships and blurred the boundaries between work and private life.

In the legal profession, the lawyer-client relationship, particularly in private practice, dictates the profession's expectations. Whether they are individuals or institutions, clients demand that lawyers provide attentive service (Heinz and Laumann, 1982; Seron, 1996) whenever it is required, even outside the normal workday. Although this has been so for a long time, clients' demands for service and availability have accelerated because lawyers can be located by phone, fax, and e-mail today wherever they are.

Technologies as social control: Computers have also created the possibility of accountability at work in a highly visible way. Trust and collegiality once provided the social foundation to ensure that tasks were completed in a timely way by professionals; a good manager's success often rested on social skills and ability to negotiate effective relations. Now lawyers' earnings derive from the billable hours they charge to clients, with machines programmed to make it possible for firms and industry to "objectively" track lawyers' time. Scott Marder, a staff attorney in the general counsel's office of a major insurance company, explained:

> The pressure was on hours—they would rotate lists of everybody's hours on a quarterly basis, how many hours you were working.... [The purpose of this was] to make you think that people were working harder than you and would be entitled to more of a raise or more of a promotion than you are.
>
> And the general counsel at the time was a fanatic about that. He had a program on the computer.... It was called "in-out." As soon as you turned on your computer, it would log you on. And, when you shut down, it would log you out. He could sit at his desk and know if you were in or out. So, everybody had their own shenanigans of putting on all of their clothes and waiting to leave and not shutting off the computer until the last split second!

The use of computers to record time at work echoes the descriptions sketched by Zuboff (1988) in her study of technology and work. She showed that where computers are used to substitute for the social tasks of supervision, a new dimension of visibility is introduced, leaving "less room for interpersonal ploys or negotiated solutions and fewer hidden corners in which to enjoy anonymous repose or indulge in overtly negative behavior" (342). As the comments of Scott Marder indicate (and Zuboff's work affirms), ploys to cover oneself do not disappear, but they may go undercover, creating a potential for lessened trust and collegiality between supervisors and staff, or those in the senior and junior ranks.

Realocation of work: Computers also have shifted to lawyers work that was formerly performed by secretarial staffs. Placing a computer on lawyers' desks was not only an invitation for them to do their own typing and drafting, but it forced them to, as private secretaries began to disappear (Murphree, 1984). As Linda Smith, a government attorney, commented in a focus group: Ten or 15 years ago, "Whoever imagined that a lawyer would ever have to type?" Another lawyer in the group, Helene Silverstein, laughed, "Do you know that federal judges were given *WordPerfect* lessons? It was quite a funny sight." Although some attorneys resisted plans to put computers on their desks because it did not look "professional," the computer became a necessary tool of the trade and a way of connecting to other colleagues. Reflecting on the transition, Deborah Stott, a general counsel at a government agency who began her career in a large firm, recalled arguing with a senior partner in his late 60s who could not understand why she needed a personal computer, or even a typewriter. Today, the sight of a computer at a professional's desk is taken for granted. It erased more of the distinctions between professionals and support personnel as lawyers became their own secretaries, answered their own phone calls, and faxed and e-mailed papers directly to their legal firms or clients. Capturing the social impact of computerization, Deborah Stott commented that "technology *does* equalize a lot of different jobs."

The expectation of clients that lawyers must turn work around faster, the ways lawyers must face new and more objectified strategies to account for that work, and the assumption that professionals will do much of their own routine work have changed the social fabric of law firms, general counsel offices in industry, and government agencies. Against this backdrop of speed-ups, visibility, and a collapse in the traditional distinction between professional and support functions, some part-timers must employ the tools of technology to create the appearance of "passing" as a full-timer, and only some have choices as to whether and to what extent they will.

Technology and the Pulls of Motherhood

As we have seen, today's part-time arrangements in large measure have been negotiated by a generation of women who seek to balance the demands of work and motherhood. While this is a good solution theoretically, conversations with these attorneys also show the ways in which social relations change when the usual expectations about availability and flexibility at work are modified.

The permeability of the boundary between work and home that is created by the "virtual" office is seen as a problem by some and a boon by others. For example, some women felt that new technology will ultimately ease the tensions facing working women. As Karen Appleby, a part-time associate in a large firm, explained,

> I have a little three-year old daughter, so I try to spend more time [with her] and go to her plays and other things. We've got a portable telephone, a telephone in the car, and a fax; you can actually get everything done.... [Attorneys] can spend a lot more time away from the office. Computers enable you to have more freedom. You can be anywhere as long as you have a fax machine and a telephone.

Vivian Scott, a lawyer in a very large corporate firm known for developing a part-time associates' program, works on a reduced schedule in the office but carries a cell phone with her and calls into the office even when she is engaged in volunteer work at her son's school on her "off days." A seasoned associate with more than a decade and a half of experience, she has a good relationship with the partners in the firm and has been given authority over associates. She also has a fax and computer at home and takes work home with her. Scott says that the boundaries between work and home are quite blurred for her, but she is pleased with the arrangement she has.

But others find the new technologies are simply too invasive, that they eat up all of their private time. Laura Adler, a lawyer in a midtown firm, describes the downside of technology:

> Fax machines made it worse.... Fedex made it worse. Cell phones; I have a cell phone now...primarily for safety...after leaving at 3:30 in the morning.... When I'm not at work I check it frequently. So, I'm not freed by the cell phone. I just have a longer tether.

Whether at work or at home, time- and labor-saving technologies may be double-edged: Though they make it easier to carry out professional obligations from a variety of locales, including home, they also make it difficult to set parameters around work, precisely because one can *always* be located. The story of the role of technology is one of paradox: Technology liberates the professional from a physical workplace; technology also, however, links the professional to the workplace at any time of any day.

Without establishing clear thresholds, there is no escape from work. At the conclusion of our interviews, attorneys were asked to complete a short survey and to report the number of hours they work from home in a typical week. Many of our interviews with part-time attorneys in large firms occurred before we sought data on hours worked at home. Of those lawyers we did question about work at home, about 14 percent work more than eight hours a week at home when they are "off work," using their equipped home offices. About half (47 percent) report working anywhere between a few and eight hours at home in a typical week, and about a third (32 percent) report that this work is limited to checking phone messages.[83] Because most respondents have decided to work part-time to take care of their children, many do strive to impose a boundary between home and work.

Taking Technology Home

Discussions with part-time lawyers from government, large firms, and industry show that they have a wide range of equipment installed at home to ease their part-time schedules, including computers (desk or laptop), faxes, modems, additional telephone lines, cellular phones, or dictation machines. While 87 percent of our respondents reported having at least one piece of equipment at home beyond a telephone, typically a desktop or laptop computer (79 percent), 13 percent reported having up to five different pieces of equipment, including computers, separate phone lines, faxes, cell phones, and dictation recorders.

Given the role of clients in the demands for lawyers' time, the amount part-timers actually do work at home and their reported use of technology varies by sector of the profession. While attorneys in government, corporations, and private practice *all* report they use the telephone and voice mail systems from home, attorneys in private firms and corporations report that they are more likely to work at home, and they rely on computers, fax machines, modems, additional phone lines, and cellular phones at home. Among government attorneys, in addition to telephone and voice mail systems, the most commonly reported machine at home is a personal computer.

The telephone and other communications technologies: In a study of solo and small-firm legal practice, Seron (1996) found that attorneys can never be far from a phone. Calls mean contact with clients and bring new clients. Calls may bring information from opposing counsel about pending cases. The reputation of an attorney often hinges on his or her demonstrative commitment to service; in practice, that means phone calls from clients must be returned promptly and thoughtfully.

Carla Fuentes, an attorney at a government agency, explained, "you have to be willing to take the phone call on your day off. You can't really say, 'Oh, I don't feel like talking to you today, it is my day off.'" Conference calls are the most common way in which these attorneys balance their part-time arrangements.[84]

While almost all report they take calls at home and regularly check their office voice mail, attorneys in government are somewhat more likely to defer a response until they return to the office, while attorneys in firms are more likely to report that they respond immediately. Carol Jacoby, an attorney at a large firm, said she encourages the people who work with her— paralegals, support staff, and clients—to call her at home: "I'm completely receptive.... My secretary always knows where I am. If there's something important she can always call me."

Voice-mail systems create the illusion of a seamless communication web and give the attorney the freedom to decide whether or not to reveal or explain one's part-time arrangement to clients. Some report that they insist on giving out their home number and underscoring to their clients that they expect to be telephoned at home. Evelyn Garth explained that she does not have a computer or access to research materials at home so that if she wants to do "any serious drafting," she has to be in her office; but she can "field calls" and "hold people's hands" from home. For attorneys in large firms, where relations with clients are particularly fostered, sophisticated telephone systems make it possible to always be in touch with the office and to ease concerns about whether one's professional commitments might be compromised when responding to the pulls of family obligations.

A recent television advertisement captures the spirit of the dilemma and suggests the advantages of cell phones for busy, working mothers. About to walk out of the house on a somewhat chaotic morning, a woman dressed in a business suit tells her children that she has "a meeting with a client." When one of her children asks, "When do I get to be a client?," she ponders how to respond. The camera catches her glancing at her cell phone, and she says, "Let's be ready for the beach in five minutes." Flash forward to a scene at the beach where the busy mom is, of course, conducting her meeting by cell phone. As the advertisement suggests, cell phones complete the chain of availability: With them, an attorney, whether full-time or part-time, can be reached at any time, almost anywhere. For the part-time lawyer, at least, the cell phone also underscores the escalation of demand for availability.

The fax machine factor: With a fax machine at home, a lawyer can, of course, receive a document at a moment's notice. A client can be patched in by telephone from work to home just as the document in question glides off. As noted above, very few government attorneys reported they have a fax machine at home; the greater reliance on them by in-house attorneys and those in law firms reflects the more permeable boundaries around work in these sectors than in government, where a fixed pattern of hours can prevent the intrusion of work into the home. [85]

Indicative of the degree to which part-timers may feel obligated to be available to the office and clients while at home, Jennifer Green, a part-timer from a large firm, explained her schedule at home this way: "I'm always keeping in touch and checking in and making sure things are done and reading things off the fax or talking to people.... There are some times when I sit down [to work] at my kitchen table for seven hours—which is fine...clients call me at home."

Underscoring the need for a fully equipped home office, Victoria Selby explained she had tried to set up a part-time schedule at home without a fax machine but found it "just too stressful to know that I had things coming into the office and that I didn't have access to them."

Telecommuting: Several of the attorneys in this study have worked out telecommuting arrangements. Two are employed by the government and three are employed as in-house counsel by a corporation. One lawyer in the LAAWS Network we spoke to had telecommuted for a firm. In most respects, the dynamics of telecommuting are very similar, if not identical, to the dynamics of part-time work. Telecommuters face similar consequences of invisibility, to point to one particular problem (Christensen, 1992).

Lorna Cartwright took on a six-month telecommuting arrangement with a firm in which one of the leaders of the LAAWS Network was a partner. She had decided to stay home after the birth of a child, but she felt lost without work. She equipped her home with a voice-mail system, installed an on-line legal research service through her computer, and worked around her son's schedule during the week, evenings and weekends. Although the original estimate was for 20 to 25 hours' work a week, she actually spent between 40 and 50 hours when the case she was working on gained speed. She reported the arrangement worked well for her although she has not had a flow of other business and has used her facilities to do *pro bono* work.

Employed as staff attorneys at the same government agency, a couple, Irene McKenzie and Joseph Jakowski, negotiated a telecommuting arrangement in order to share work and child care. The couple set up a fully equipped office in their home and were given the software to connect with the government agency for which they worked. Conditions were ripe for their wish to telecommute because their agency was concerned that it would lose the budget allocations for their positions if they left and there is a presidential mandate to make the federal workplace more family friendly through a special National Telecommuting Initiative. (Their contract stipulated that they would have child care on the days they worked at home and that with reasonable notice they would accept a site visit to check their home office.) While Irene described her concerns, choices, and ambivalence in much the same way as other women part-timers, Joseph's decision to telecommute was a deviation from most men's patterns. Joseph Jakowski's decision suggests that there is no *a priori* reason why alternative work arrangements must remain a "woman's solution" to the need to share work and family time.

PART VI

CONCLUSION

CHAPTER 15

CONCLUSION

Part-time work arrangements in the legal profession are seen as a solution to the work/family time dilemmas faced by many lawyers in their child-rearing years. Most lawyers who work on these alternative schedules are women, because women are normatively more free to choose to do so and because child care, considered to be women's responsibility, is the most commonly accepted justification for granting part-time schedules. Despite the fact that women attorneys are a significant and growing proportion of the profession, part-time work is neither typical nor common.

This study shows the benefits and pitfalls of part-time status for lawyers and the institutions they work for. Reluctance to ask for part-time schedules, and the resistance of employers to grant it, have to do not only with the practical problems of coordination and economics but go to the heart of what it means to be a true professional. In law, as in other professions, commitment and excellence are often measured by the seemingly unlimited number of hours practitioners work, indicating that their first priority is their vocation. Practitioners who work circumscribed hours are considered to be "time deviants." Although the "greediness" of different spheres of law varies, the norms demanding constant availability of the individual lawyer persist, especially in private sector law firms, where they have become even more pronounced in today's competitive environment. Thus, even as part-time work is becoming institutionalized because of the profession's growing awareness of the problems lawyers have in integrating family and work lives, and of their discontent with *escalating* time demands, part-time work is often stigmatized for its violation of the profession's norm.

Technology is part of the problem because it speeds the pace of practice with rapid turnaround times that are created and enforced by the use of computers, fax machines, cell telephones, and other devices. However, it is also part of the solution because it permits part-timers to work effectively at sites outside the office. Here too, new problems arise as the boundary between work and home life becomes blurred.

While much of the focus of this research has been on the experiences of individuals, alternative work arrangements pose both advantages and disadvantages for the organizations permitting them. Part-time work options are a way to attract or keep legal talent, and in a profession in which women make up an increasingly large proportion of practitioners, it has become less possible to ignore their desires to be responsive to contending commitments at home and at work. Indeed, the government sector uses defined part-time policies to attract a level of legal talent and experience that would not be otherwise available. Because it is usually lawyers with a number of years of experience who desire part-time work, these arrangements save organizations from losing substantial investments in attorneys they have trained.

Part-time status has career consequences. Most part-timers appear to be blocked from promotion into supervisory or partnership positions. Indeed, most of the attorneys in this study agreed this is a *quid pro quo* for their withdrawal from a full-time commitment and, while disappointed, they felt it is reasonable and understandable from the standpoint of the organization. With such understandings in place, all sectors of the legal workplace may employ the talents of experienced lawyers without having to commit to the career progression of part-time attorneys or acquire obligations to them. Of course, there are consequences for the organizations in terms of lower commitment. For the part-timers who return to full-time work, however, it is possible to go back on track, although they may lose years of seniority.

Part-time arrangements may also pose difficulties for the internal life of organizations. Norms of professionalism require a commitment to contribute to the quality of work life of the organization; and attorneys, like all professionals, are expected to be good colleagues. Without time to socialize and communicate informally, part-time arrangements compromise an intangible but essential part of collegial life—the camaraderie and social bonds that create high morale and a sociable place to work.

A firm's reputation is in part contingent on its contribution to the collegial life of the profession at large. Because they place limits on their hours of work, part-timers are rarely able to contribute to this aspect of the professional calling. For example, part-timers are less available to share in responsibilities for bar association activities, in training and mentoring of younger colleagues, or in expanding the knowledge base of the profession by studying and writing on professional matters.

While many part-timers bring sophisticated legal expertise to their work they rarely have the time to develop the social ties necessary for effective client development, although some have acquired client loyalty in past full-time work. In an increasingly competitive market for legal services, this may be a serious shortcoming.

Finally, because the number of part-timers in any one organization remains small, there is little pressure for change in administrative or personnel rules to address their needs. Should part-time arrangements become more common, however, the profession will have to answer the growing number of questions about part-time seniority, remuneration, pensions, benefits, and promotion.

Lawyers who make policy in their organizations have differing views about the feasibility of alternative work arrangements. The federal government has worked out formal guidelines to provide solutions to some of the problems of part-time employment for their lawyers, and the more defined government work schedules make it possible to implement them when they are supported by the positive attitudes of supervising attorneys. The private sector faces different kinds of challenges, and the mind-sets of the top people are also crucial. Although management committees of large law firms are concerned about losing young lawyers who resist the workaholic demands that intrude on their family lives, there does not seem to be great interest in strengthening arrangements for part-time work. Some firms see such changes as inevitable given the attrition rates of associates. Some believe no changes will take place until men begin to pressure firms for more flexible schedules, a "solution" that others hold to be unlikely because of the costs of breaking with tradition and the competitive pressures facing the legal world today. Some others believe change may come when women partners commonly participate in the management of large firms. Yet because there are still so few women partners, and because they have less power than male partners, most did not believe they could accomplish serious change. Further, as we have seen, not all women partners agree on the feasibility of part-time work. Yet, sympathies of women clients—women are now a rising number of directors of corporate legal departments—could encourage firms to accept more flexibility, according to some other attorneys.

Now that part-time work schedules are a growing option, the profession at large should address its traditional stereotypes about what is required to be a successful practitioner. Senior attorneys in large firms, who came of professional age in a different era, need to accept a new model of the excellent attorney, one that includes the many younger attorneys who are deeply committed to their work *and* to their families and the part-time attorneys who have decided *not* to leave their profession. While old sterotypes tend to linger on the screen of social life, it is time for the profession to acknowledge that one may be both a dedicated professional and a dedicated family member.

We may expect that changes in the law profession's existing power structures and the willingness of men to join with their women colleagues in challenging the prevailing order will result in legitimation of greater workplace flexibility. Resolutions of conflicting pressures will be difficult, however, since the issue of work hours goes far beyond its immediate importance to lawyers seeking change and those who manage the legal workplace. Long hours of work and visibility of effort have symbolic meaning, and serve as proxies for commitment and excellence. Long hours of work also bond professionals socially as well as professionally, placing those who are not always "there" in a marginal position. Furthermore, the gendered nature of part-time work is a reflection of strong cultural values about the proper roles of the two sexes and the division of labor in society. These are values and conditions that are not easy to disrupt, and they make the question of part-time work contested terrain and a proxy for many issues beyond lawyers' work schedules.

PART VII

APPENDICES

APPENDIX A

RESEARCH METHODOLOGY

An Overview of This Research

The study on which this book is based was designed to determine the experiences lawyers have had with part-time work in the legal profession. It was funded by the Alfred P. Sloan Foundation as part of a larger initiative to identify problems and issues related to the integration of family and work by professionals in modern society. This study explored the question in several different spheres of the legal profession—private law firms, corporation legal departments (in-house lawyers), and government—to identify how different work structures and cultures respond to alternative work patterns. We examined the following themes to understand the impact of part-time work arrangements on the career patterns of lawyers:

1. The scheduling of work and home responsibilities, including the use of surrogate child care;
2. The role of management in the implementation of part-time work arrangements, including the use of standard policies to guide decision-making or the negotiation of customized arrangements;
3 The impact of part-time arrangements on lawyers' promotions and career mobility;
4. The relationship between part-time arrangements and organizations' cultures, focusing on whether and to what extent part-timers are marginalized from the centers of activity and decision-making.

Because there is no census of part-time lawyers and because some lawyers who work full-time have worked part time in the past, we used a snowball sample to identify lawyers in various spheres of the profession.

To discover the impact of part-time work arrangements on the career trajectories of the individuals and organizations involved, we (1) conducted open-ended interviews with a snowball sample of part-time lawyers and (2) conducted informant interviews with some managers of part-timers and full-time colleagues of part-timers. The interviews were conducted between 1994 and 1996. All interviews were conducted using a common protocol of questions, but respondents's comments also shaped the direction of each conversation and the themes emerging from it. Most interviews with working lawyers, both part-time and full-time, were conducted in their offices; those with attorneys who were on leave or unemployed were conducted in their homes. Each interview was taped and transcribed.

We also developed a questionnaire that was left with respondents, with the request that they fill it out and mail it to us. This asked for personal background data including their marital status, approximate family and individual income, number and age of children, and type of child-care provision. We received 84 questionnaires back from the 105 lawyers with part-time work experience who were interviewed for this study. (These numbers do not include the lawyers interviewed for a previous study of large-firm lawyers, whose interviews were used for this study as well. See Table 17.1, Appendix C.) Of the 105 lawyers, 62 answered questions about their use of technology.

Identifying the Sample

As noted in the introduction to this book, we obtained names of part-time lawyers in private firms and corporations from our contacts at the Association of the Bar of the City of New York's Lawyers for the Advancement of Alternative Work Schedules Network. We also drew on personal contacts with lawyers we knew. Other sources included interviews with large-firm attorneys for a study of eight large corporate law firms conducted by Epstein *et al.* (1995), lawyers currently on part-time schedules at the partner rank, and associates above the fifth-year level. The sample of part-timer associates in small firms came from contacts made at the LAAWS Network with a subset drawn from Seron's study of lawyers who run part-time solo firm practices (1996). Corporation counsels were located from references by large-firm lawyers and personal contacts. To obtain names of individuals who work on a part-time arrangement in government, we contacted a professional association composed of the General Counsels of all federal agencies in New York City. Using this list, we carried out a mail survey to these counsels about the numbers of attorneys employed in various kinds of alternative work arrangements. The survey also inquired as to whether the counsels would be willing to permit us to interview attorneys in their offices. Prior to fielding interviews with government attorneys in federal offices, we conducted a focus group with general counsels about their experiences with this arrangement. We also obtained permission from the general counsel's office of a major agency of the city of New York to interview attorneys.

We also used a survey conducted by the LAAWS Network of lawyers interested in part-time work (Schwab, 1994) or currently practicing as part-time lawyers, following up with lawyers who expressed interest in being interviewed.

Because all interviewees were guaranteed confidentiality, as outlined in guidelines for scientific research on human subjects, the names of agencies, industries, and firms cannot be identified. Indeed, the assurance of confidentiality was an important factor in obtaining cooperation to conduct this study.

A Profile of the Sample

The sample interviewed for this study totaled 125 attorneys. These lawyers were drawn from 32 private firms, seven government agencies, and 11 corporations. It included some lawyers who had worked part-time and had been laid off from their jobs, as well as those presently working reduced schedules.

The sample included 105 lawyers who were working part-time at the time of their interviews or who had worked part-time in the recent past. Twenty lawyers worked full-time and had no part-time experience, but reported on their relationships with part-timers. Among the part-timers were 18 lawyers working in-house at corporations; 32 in government agencies; and 41 in private law firms. Twelve lawyers in solo practice worked part-time at home. One lawyer worked for a nonprofit legal service.

Ten lawyers in supervisory positions were interviewed for their perspectives on policies and practices concerning alternative work schedules at their organizations; six of them currently were part-time partners. Fifteen full-time attorneys were interviewed about their experiences working with part-time colleagues. Two of the full-time attorneys had telecommuting arrangements, two worked full-time on a compressed work schedule offered by the federal government, working longer hours on nine business days with a tenth one off, and one was a temporary contractual employee. In addition to the figures reported in Table 17.1 (see Appendix C), we conducted a focus group with six heads of general counsel offices in federal agencies to understand how they managed alternative work arrangements. (We interviewed one in depth for the study.)

Most of the lawyers in this study who had part-time experience were white women. We were able to locate and interview only seven men working a reduced work schedule. We interviewed three African-American lawyers, all women working part time for the government, four Asian women, and a Latino man.[86]

We located a small number of lawyers with supervisory or executive titles who had held part-time positions or who were currently working part-time. Eight were partners in private firms, five of them in large corporate firms; seven members of this group had part-time schedules while partners and one had been part-time as an associate and switched to full-time work before becoming partner. Only one in-house administrator with the title of assistant general counsel was part-time. Four supervisors from government agencies are part-time.

To develop a fuller, more nuanced understanding of the impact of part-time arrangements on the culture and organization of legal practices, we conducted informal interviews with a number of managers and full-time colleagues at work sites where we conducted interviews with part-timers.

All of these interviews were conducted with the aim of providing information on a range of experiences with part-time lawyering in the three principal legal domains within the limits of our time and financial budgets.

PART-TIME WORK
POLICIES AND ISSUES
THEY COVER

The demand for part-time work and the discussions and debates about it in the legal profession during the last few years have resulted in a variety of alternative work arrangements. Some employers have established policies, and some have worked out arrangements on a case-by-case basis.

In 1993 the Committee on Women in the Profession of the Association of the Bar of the City of New York undertook a study of these policies and of the needs and experiences of attorneys who had negotiated new work arrangements (Schwab, 1994) or who were interested in doing so.

The study listed a range of part-time and alternative arrangements that have been established in the legal workplace, many of them exemplified by lawyers interviewed for this book:

■ *Part-time work:* A part-time schedule is one with reduced hours compared to the norm in the sector. In some cases, part-time work is arranged on a project-by-project basis.

■ *Job sharing:* Some organizations permit two individuals to share one job and its salary and benefits. In job-sharing arrangements it is often left to the individuals involved to work out the division of labor and to be responsible for ensuring that all work demands are covered.

■ *Telecommuting:* In a telecommuting arrangement, the individual may work a full-time schedule, but part of the work is done at home. The arrangement often requires the person to connect from home to the office's communications and computer technologies.

■ *Phased retirement:* As retirement approaches, some employees are allowed to gradually reduce the number of hours worked. In the legal profession, this option is particularly common in private firms among senior males who are encouraged to curtail their commitments over time, including their business development activities, and are given the title of counsel.

■ *Flextime:* In a flextime arrangement, organizations differentiate between core hours when all employees must be on the premises and "flex hours" when employees may exercise options about which hours they will work. This option is more typical in government, where normal working hours tend to be more regulated than they are in the private sector.

■ *Compressed workweek:* Particularly common in the government, a compressed workweek allows employees to work full-time hours in less than a full-time workweek. In the federal government, for example, employees may work 80 hours over nine business days, with the tenth day off. In effect, this schedule gives employees alternating two-day and three-day weekends.

Part-Time Policies and Negotiations

■ *Law firms and corporations:* Most law firms and corporate in-house legal departments do *not* have formal written policies on part-time work. Some provide general statements referring to part-time work as a possible option but do not have detailed policies. In some in-house settings, part-time work policy usually is folded into broader work/family initiatives. When no part-time policy of any sort exists, lawyers have often taken the initiative to negotiate pioneering arrangements.

■ *Government:* The highly variable character of part-time policy in law firms and corporations contrasts with the situation in government agencies subject to federal, state, or city guidelines for flexible work schedules. While chief counsels have some discretion over which alternative arrangements are implemented in their agencies' offices, part-time options tend to be codified in formal policies that make part-time work a legitimate and accepted alternative to full-time work.

Issues Covered by Part-Time Arrangements

- *Eligibility:* Part-time work is rarely an option for new law graduates. Often it is understood, if not stipulated, that a person should have worked in an organization for at least a few years to establish eligibility for part-time scheduling. Occasionally, lawyers are *hired* on a part-time basis after some years of full-time legal experience. These usually fall in three categories: (1) those who enter firms laterally or as a result of merger agreements; (2) those hired to fill a discrete function for which a full-time person is not needed; and (3) lawyers brought in on temporary assignments through contract agencies.

- *Acceptable reasons for part-time work:* The prevailing understanding in most organizations is that part-time work is sought for reasons related to child rearing. In a few instances, this is specified in written policy. Other reasons for which part-time work may be granted include medical problems and disabilities, infirmity during pregnancy, and time to tend to other family needs (*e.g.,* to care for a sick family member). Though it is very atypical, permission to reduce hours is sometimes granted to attorneys who want time to pursue outside interests such as political activity or artistic endeavors.

- *Number and regularity of days or hours worked:* Most part-time arrangements stipulate that employees work three or four days a week, or a corresponding number of hours per week (*e.g.,* "80 percent time"). There is, however, a great deal of variation in the number of working hours expected within a day, the start and end times of the workday, and the degree of schedule constancy expected from week to week.

  In large firms, part-time arrangements may also include annual billable hours requirements, calculated as a percentage of the firm's yearly standard for full-time attorneys. Because yearly standards vary by firm, their definitions of billable hours for part-time attorneys vary as well. According to Epstein *et al.* (1995), annual billable hours range from 1,800 to 3,000.

- *Compensation:* The most common compensation scheme for part-time attorneys is a salary proportionate to the percentage of hours worked. Frequently, this is a direct relationship (*e.g.,* an 80 percent salary for working on an 80 percent schedule). In small or midsize firms, part-time salary sometimes is decreased by an additional 5 percent or so to cover the costs of additional overhead.

  Given the small number of law firm partners who are part-timers, no clear pattern has emerged on parameters for their sharing in firm profits.

Whether part-time attorneys are offered the option of becoming equity or non-equity partners seems to depend on a number of factors, including their business development potential.

■ *Benefits:* Medical and life insurance benefits of part-time attorneys are usually the same as those provided for lawyers working full time. Their pensions, however, may be modified. The length of time one must work to be vested in a pension system may be extended, while pension values may accrue at a slower pace. Benefits for part-time employees are also subject to state and federal regulation and requirements.

■ *Bonuses and awards:* There are few conventions about whether part-time attorneys are eligible for bonuses. On occasion, bonuses are proffered on a proportional basis, much like salaries by some firms and in-house departments. More often, bonus eligibility is unclear, as is the basis for calculating amounts. Government agencies vary as well as to whether part-time attorneys are eligible for merit awards given to exemplary employees.

■ *Quality of assignments:* Although it is not common, policies may contain a clause about the quality of work assignments a part-time lawyer can expect. One such policy stated that the attorney "will be provided with important and interesting assignments commensurate with his or her experience and skills that can be performed satisfactorily on the proposed part-time schedule." Usually, part-time attorneys are not given time-sensitive, high-profile matters, and will not be the lead attorney on most of their cases. There is variation, however, on whether they are involved in supervision of junior colleagues.

■ *Expectations regarding work overflow:* Some agreements caution attorneys that they must remain flexible to work demands, if necessary working longer hours on any given day, taking work home in the evenings, coming into the office on weekends, and relinquishing part-time status temporarily to attend to emergencies or especially intensive cases. Compensatory time is available on a formal basis in government agencies; in firms and corporations, attorneys tend to make up for overtime informally.

■ *Child-care arrangements:* Many part-time agreements stipulate that alternative child care must be arranged to guarantee the attorney's ability to work on his or her off days should the need arise. To this end, firms may even make full-time child care a condition of granting a part-time schedule. Telecommuters may also be asked to show proof that child-care service is arranged.

- *Length of time a person may work part time:* Agreements vary about how long an attorney can work part-time. Most organizations regard part-time work as temporary, and some cap its duration at two years, linking it to their beliefs about mothers' requirements in the early years of child care. Frequently, however, attorneys work part-time longer than two years; and firms with the two-year limit often permit extensions.

- *Promotion and career advancement:* The key policy issues related to promotion and career advancement for part-time attorneys center on (1) whether one may be promoted while part-time; (2) the length of time one must wait after resuming a full-time schedule to be considered for promotion; and (3) whether progress toward promotion is waived while working part-time. For the most part, agreements reflect an understanding that attorneys lose promotion opportunities while they are part-time and regain them after returning to full-time status. Even then, apart from government agencies, which delineate seniority and promotion steps, an organization rarely states how long an attorney must work before being eligible for promotion. Only in exceptional cases do part-time agreements foreclose promotion options completely.

- *Options to return full-time:* Though part-time work is usually treated as temporary, options to return to full-time are not always automatic. In government agencies, this is contingent on the availability of job or salary lines (known as "FTEs" or full-time equivalents). Still, there is more fluidity in government than in law firms or in-house departments in terms of being able to move back and forth between full-time and part-time schedules. Since the part-time attorneys we interviewed often wish to remain on part-time schedules indefinitely, it is not clear what patterns will emerge when and if they choose to return to full-time work.

APPENDIX C

TABLES*

*Table numbers refer to chapter number and number of table in the chapter

TABLE 17.1* PROFILE OF ATTORNEYS IN STUDY

Work Status	Large Firms		Other Firms		Corporate Legal Departments		Government Agencies		Solo Practices	Totals
	Partner	Associate	Partner	Associate	Supervisor	Non-Supervisor	Supervisor	Non-Supervisor		
Currently Part-time	4 (5%)	26 (33%)	2 (3%)	1 (1%)	0	12 (15%)	4 (5%)	17 (22%)	12 (15%)	78 (100%)
Formerly Part-time	1 (4%)	4 (15%)	1 (4%)	3 (11%)	1 (4%)	5 (19%)	0	12 (44%)	0	27 (100%)
Never Part-time	0	0	0	0	0	2 (10%)	12 (60%)	6 (30%)	0	20 (100%)
Totals	5 (4%)	30 (24%)	3 (2%)	4 (3%)	1 (1%)	19 (15%)	16 (13%)	35 (28%)	12 (10%)	125 (100%)

Sector of Law

N=125

Percentages run across columns and may not equal 100 due to rounding.
*The table includes five heads of general counsel offices of federal agencies who were interviewed only in a focus group and had never worked part time.

TABLE 6.1 INDIVIDUAL INCOME

Employment Status	In Thousands of Dollars									Totals
	Less than 15	15 to 30	31 to 50	51 to 75	76 to 100	101 to 150	151 to 250	251 to 750	More than 750	
Currently Part-time	4 (7%)	2 (4%)	12 (22%)	8 (15%)	11 (20%)	11 (20%)	3 (5%)	2 (4%)	2 (4%)	55 (100%)
Currently Full-time	0	0	0	8 (40%)	4 (20%)	3 (15%)	5 (25%)	0	0	20 (100%)
Totals	4 (5%)	2 (3%)	12 (16%)	16 (21%)	15 (20%)	14 (19%)	8 (11%)	2 (3%)	2 (3%)	75 (100%)

N=75
Percentages run across columns and may not equal 100 due to rounding.
Source: Demographic Data Sheets

TABLE 6.2 INDIVIDUAL INCOME BY LEGAL SECTOR

Employment Status and Legal Sector	In Thousands of Dollars									Totals
	Less than 15	15 to 30	31 to 50	51 to 75	76 to 100	101 to 150	151 to 250	251 to 750	More than 750	
Part-time Private Firm	0	0	1 (4%)	2 (8%)	6 (23%)	10 (38%)	3 (12%)	2 (8%)	2 (8%)	26 (100%)
Full-time Private Firm	0	0	0	0	0	1 (25%)	3 (75%)	0	0	4 (100%)
Part-time Legal Dept.	0	0	1 (10%)	3 (30%)	5 (50%)	1 (10%)	0	0	0	10 (100%)
Full-time Legal Dept.	0	0	0	0	1 (33%)	0	2 (67%)	0	0	3 (100%)
Part-time Government	0	2 (13%)	10 (67%)	3 (20%)	0	0	0	0	0	15 (100%)
Full-time Government	0	0	0	8 (62%)	3 (23%)	2 (15%)	0	0	0	13 (100%)
Part-time Solo Practice	4 (100%)	0	0	0	0	0	0	0	0	4 (100%)
Totals	4 (5%)	2 (3%)	12 (16%)	16 (21%)	15 (20%)	14 (19%)	8 (11%)	2 (3%)	2 (3%)	75 (100%)

N=75
Percentages run across columns and may not equal 100 due to rounding. Source: Demographic Data Sheets

TABLE 13.0 SPOUSES' OCCUPATION

Lawyer's Work Status	Occupation								
	Attorney	Finance	Engineer	Academic	Accountant	Doctor	Sales	Other Professional	Non-Professional	Totals
Currently Part-time	30 (49%)	9 (15%)	4 (7%)	3 (5%)	3 (5%)	3 (5%)	1 (2%)	5 (8%)	3 (5%)	61 (100%)
Currently Full-time	7 (37%)	1 (5%)	1 (5%)	1 (5%)	0	0	1 (5%)	6 (32%)	2 (11%)	19 (100%)
Totals	37 (46%)	10 (13%)	5 (6%)	4 (5%)	3 (4%)	3 (4%)	2 (3%)	11 (14%)	5 (6%)	80 (100%)

N=80
Percentages run across columns and may not equal 100 due to rounding.
Source: Demographic Data Sheets

TABLE 13.1 FAMILY SIZE

	Number of Children					
Work Status	0	1	2	3	4	Totals
Currently Part-time	5 (8%)	15 (24%)	36 (58%)	5 (8%)	1 (2%)	62 (100%)
Currently Full-time	3 (14%)	5 (23%)	12 (55%)	2 (9%)	0	22 (100%)
Totals	8 (10%)	20 (24%)	48 (57%)	7 (8%)	1 (1%)	84 (100%)

N=84
Percentages run across columns and may not equal 100 due to rounding.
Source: Demographic Data Sheets

TABLE 13.2 CHILD-CARE ARRANGEMENTS

	Type of Provider					
Work Status	Full-time/ Live-in	Part-time	Baby-sitter	Relative	Day Care	Totals
Currently Part-time	28 (50%)	20 (36%)	4 (7%)	3 (5%)	1 (2%)	56 (100%)
Currently Full-time	4 (31%)	2 (15%)	3 (23%)	0	4 (31%)	13 (100%)
Totals	32 (46%)	22 (32%)	7 (10%)	3 (4%)	5 (7%)	69 (100%)

N=69
Percentages run across columns and may not equal 100 due to rounding.
Source: Demographic Data Sheets

TABLE 13.3 CHILD-CARE ARRANGEMENTS AND FAMILY INCOME

Family Income in Thousands of Dollars	Type of Child Care					
	Full-time/Live-in	Part-time	Baby-sitter	Relative	Day Care	Totals
76 to 100	0	3 (33%)	3 (33%)	1 (11%)	2 (22%)	9 (100%)
101 to 150	4 (27%)	6 (40%)	1 (6%)	1 (6%)	3 (20%)	15 (100%)
151 to 250	10 (53%)	7 (37%)	2 (11%)	0	0	19 (100%)
251 to 400	10 (83%)	1 (8%)	0	1 (8%)	0	12 (100%)
More than 400	5 (100%)	0	0	0	0	5 (100%)
Totals	29 (48%)	17 (28%)	6 (10%)	3 (5%)	5 (8%)	60 (100%)

N=60
Percentages run across columns and may not equal 100 due to rounding.
Source: Demographic Data Sheets

TABLE 13.4   CHILD-CARE ARRANGEMENTS AND SPOUSE'S OCCUPATION

Type of Child Care	Occupation									
	Attorney	Finance	Engineer	Academic	Accountant	Doctor	Sales	Other Profession	Non-Profession	Totals
Full-Time/Live-in	17 (53%)	5 (16%)	3 (9%)	0	1 (3%)	1 (3%)	2 (6%)	2 (6%)	1 (3%)	32 (100%)
Part-time	13 (65%)	2 (10%)	0	2 (10%)	0	0	0	2 (10%)	1 (5%)	20 (100%)
Baby-sitter	0	2 (29%)	1 (14%)	0	0	0	0	3 (43%)	1 (14%)	7 (100%)
Relative	2 (67%)	1 (33%)	0	0	0	0	0	0	0	3 (100%)
Day Care	3 (60%)	0	0	0	0	0	0	1 (20%)	1 (20%)	5 (100%)
Totals	35 (52%)	10 (15%)	4 (6%)	2 (3%)	1 (1%)	1 (1%)	2 (3%)	8 (12%)	4 (6%)	67 (100%)

N=64
Percentages run across columns and may not equal 100 due to rounding.
Source: Demographic Data Sheets

BIBLIOGRAPHY

Abbott, Andrew. 1989a. *The System of Professions.* Chicago: University of Chicago Press.
————. 1989b. "The New Occupational Structure." *Work and Occupations* 16, 3 (August).
Abel, Richard L., and Philip S.C. Lewis. 1989. *Lawyers in Society: Comparative Theories.* Berkeley: University of California Press.
American Bar Association, Young Lawyers Division. 1991. *The State of the Legal Profession, 1990.* Chicago, American Bar Foundation.
Auchincloss, Louis. 1956. *The Great World and Timothy Colt.* Boston: Houghton Mifflin.
————. 1974. *The Partners.* Boston: Houghton Mifflin.

Barnett, Rosalind, and Caryl Rivers. 1996. *She Works, He Works: How Two-Income Families Are Happier, Healthier and Better Off.* San Francisco: HarperCollins.
————. 1997. "Bashing Working Families." *Dissent* (Fall): 13–15.
Beck, Susan. 1997. "High Five." *California Lawyer* (June): 31–36.
Becker, Gary Stanley. 1964. *Human Capital: A Theoretical and Empirical Analysis.* New York: National Bureau of Economic Research.
————. 1976. *The Economic Approach to Human Behavior.* Chicago: University of Chicagp Press.
Becker, Howard. 1963. *Outsiders: Studies in the Sociology of Deviance.* London: Free Press.
Beechey, V., and T. Perkins. 1987. *A Matter of Hours: Women, Part-Time Work and the Labour Market.* Cambridge: Polity Press.
Blank, Rebecca M. 1990. "Understanding Part-Time Work." *Research in Labor Economies,* vol II, 137–158.
Bok, Derek Curtis. 1993. *The Cost of Talent: How Executives and Professionals Are Paid and How It Affects America.* New York: Free Press.
Bourdieu, Pierre. [1972] 1977. *Outline of a Theory of Practice.* London: Cambridge University Press.
Bremner, Robert H. 1985. "The New Deal and Social Welfare." In *Fifty Years Later: The New Deal Evaluated,* ed. Harvard Sitkoff, 69–92. New York: McGraw-Hill.
Bureau of Labor Statistics, Department of Labor. 1997. *Employment & Earnings* 44:1.
Buswell, C., and S. Jenkins. 1994. "Equal Opportunity Policies, Employment and Patriarchy." *Gender, Work, and Organization* 1(2): 83–93.
Byrne, Noel T. 1988. "Time Deviance." Paper presented at the annual meetings of the American Sociological Association, Atlanta, Georgia, August.

Caplan, Lincoln. 1993. *Skadden.* New York: Farrar, Straus, Giroux.
Card, David, and Alan B. Krueger. 1995. *Myth and Measurement: The New Economics of the Minimum Wage.* Princeton, NJ: Princeton University Press.
Carr-Saunders, A. M. and P. A. Wilson. 1993. *The Professions.* Oxford: Clarendon Press.

Chambers, David L. 1989. "Accommodation and Satisfaction: Women and Men Lawyers and the Balance of Work and Family." *Law and Social Inquiry* 14(2): 251–287.

Christensen, Kathleen. 1992. "Managing Invisible Employees: How to Meet the Telecommuting Challenge." *Employment Relations Today* (Summer): 133–143.

Collinson, David L., and Margaret Collinson. 1997. "Delayering Managers:Time-Space Surveillance and Its Gendered Effects." *Organization* 4(3): 375–407.

Coltrane, Scott. 1996. *Family Man: Fatherhood, Housework, and Gender Equity.* New York: Oxford University Press.

Coser, Lewis A. 1974. *Greedy Institutions: Patterns of Undivided Commitment.* New York: Free Press.

Coser, Lewis, and Rose Laub Coser. 1963. "Time Perspectives and Social Structure." In *Modern Sociology,* ed. A.W. Gouldner and H.P. Gouldner, 638–650. New York: Harcourt Brace Jovanovich.

———— 1974. "The Housewife and Her Greedy Family." In Lewis, Coser *Greedy Institutions,* 89–100. New York: Free Press.

Curran, Barbara, and Clara N. Carson. 1991. *Supplement to the Lawyer Statistical Report: The U.S. Legal Profession in 1988.* Chicago: American Bar Foundation.

————. 1994. *The Lawyer Statistical Report: The U.S. Legal Profession in the 1990s.* Chicago: American Bar Foundation.

Davis, Kingsley, and Wilbert E. Moore. 1945. "Some Principles of Stratification." *American Sociological Review* 10: 242–249.

de Grazia, Sebastian. 1962. *Of Time, Work and Leisure.* New York: Twentieth Century Fund.

DiTomaso, Nancy. 1996. "The Loose Coupling of Jobs: The Subcontracting of Everyone?" Paper presented at the annual meetings of the American Sociological Association, Washington, D.C., August.

Dixon, Jo, and Carroll Seron. 1995. "Stratification in the Legal Profession: Sex, Sector and Salary." *Law & Society Review* 29: 401–432.

Durkheim, Emile. [1893] 1933. *The Division of Labor in Society.* New York: Free Press.

Edwards, Richard. 1979. *Contested Terrain: The Transformation of the Workplace in the Twentieth Century.* New York: Basic Books.

England, Paula, and George Farkas. 1986. *Households Employment and Gender: A Social, Economic and Demographic View.* New York: Aldine.

Epstein, Cynthia Fuchs. 1970. *Woman's Place: Options and Limits in Professional Careers.* Berkeley: University of California Press.

————. 1987. "Multiple Demands and Multiple Roles." In *Spouse, Parent Worker: On Gender and Multiple Roles,* ed. Faye Crosby. New Haven:Yale University Press.

————. 1988. *Deceptive Distinctions.* New Haven:Yale University Press.

————. 1991. "The Nonwork Aspects of Work." *The Antioch Review* (Winter): 4–55.

————. [1981] 1993. *Women in Law.* Chicago: University of Illinois Press.

————. 1997. "Multiple Myths and Outcomes of Sex Segregation." *New Tork Law School Journal of Human Rights.* 14(1): 185–210.

Epstein, Cynthia Fuchs, Robert Sauté, Bonnie Oglensky, and Martha Gever. 1995.

"Glass Ceilings and Open Doors: Women's Mobility in the Legal Profession." *Fordham Law Review* 64(2): 291–449.

Faludi, Susan. 1991. *Backlash*. New York: Crown.

Fiore, Faye. 1997. "Full-Time Moms a Minority Now, Census Bureau Finds." *Los Angeles Times*, Nov. 26, 1.

Foucault, Michel. 1979. *Discipline and Punish*. Trans. Alan Sheridan. New York: Vintage Books.

France, Mike. 1994. "Non-Equity Status Becoming Increasingly Popular in Firms." *National Law Journal* (Oct. 3): C3.

Freidson, Eliot, 1986. *Professional Powers: A Study of the Institutionalization of Formal Knowledge*. Chicago: University of Chicago Press.

———. 1992. "Professionalism as Model and Ideology." In *Lawyers' Ideals/Lawyers' Practices: Transformations in the American Legal Profession*, ed. Robert Nelson, David Trubek, and Rayman Solomon, 215–229. Ithaca: Cornell University Press.

Gabriel, Yiannis. 1993. "Organizational Nostalgia—Reflections on 'The Golden Age.' " In *Emotions in Organizations*, ed. Stephen Fineman, 118-141. London: Sage Publications.

———. 1997. "An Introduction to the Social Psychology of Insults in Organizations." Paper presented at the annual Symposium of the International Society for the Psychoanalytic Study of Organizations, Philadelphia.

Galanter, Marc, and Thomas Palay. 1991. *Tournament of Lawyers: The Transformation of the Big Law Firm*. Chicago: University of Chicago Press.

———. 1992. "The Transormation of the Big Law Firm." In *Lawyers' Ideals/Lawyers' Practices: Transformations in the American Legal Profession*, ed. Robert Nelson, David Trubek, and Raymon Solomon, 31–62. Ithica: Cornell University Press.

Gallagher, Maggie, 1998. "Warning: May Be Harmful to Children: Day Careless." *National Review*, Vol. L, No. 1 (Jan. 26): 37–43.

Geary, Robert. 1997. "Nanny in Tot Sex Horror: Dad Catches Her Act on Hidden Camera Says Cops." (N.Y.) *Daily News*, Dec. 4, 7.

Gilson, Ronald J., and Robert H. Mnookin. 1985. "Sharing Among the Human Capitalists: An Economic Inquiry into the Corporate Law Firm and How Partners Split Profits." *Stanford Law Review* 37(2): 313–390.

———. 1989. "Coming of Age in a Corporate Law Firm: The Economics of Associate Career Patterns." *Stanford Law Review* 41: 567–595.

Goffman, Erving. 1952. "On Cooling the Mark Out: Some Aspects of Adaptation to Failure." As reprinted in *The Pleasures of Sociology*, 1980, edited and with an introduction by Lewis A. Coser. New York: New American Library.

———. 1959. *The Presentation of Self in Everyday Life*. New York: Doubleday.

———. 1961. *Asylums: Essays on the Social Situation of Mental Patients and Other Inmates*. New York: Doubleday.

———. 1963. *Stigma: Notes on the Management of Spoiled Identity*. Englewood Cliffs, NJ: Prentice Hall.

Goode, William J. 1957. "Community Within a Community: The Professions." *American Sociological Review* 22: 194-200.

———. 1973. "The Theoretical Limits of Professionalization." In *Explorations in Social Theory*, 341–382. New York: Oxford University Press.

————. 1979. *The Celebration of Heroes: Prestige as a Control System.* Berkeley: University of California Press.

Gornick, Hanet C., and Jerry A. Jacobs. 1995. "A Cross-National Analysis of the Wages of Part-Time Workers: Evidence from the United States, the United Kingdom, Canada and Australia. Unpublished manuscript.

———— 1996. "A Cross-National Analysis of the Wages of Part-Time Workers: Evidence from the United States, the United Kingdom, Canada and Australia." *Work, Employment and Society* 10(1): 1–27.

Goulden, Joseph. 1971. *The Super-Lawyers.* New York: Dell.

Gouldner, Alvin W. 1960. "The Norms of Reciprocity: A Preliminary Statement," *American Sociological Review* 25 (April): 161–178.

Granfield, Robert. 1992. *Making Elite Lawyers.* New York: Routledge.

Gray, John. 1992. *Men Are From Mars, Women Are From Venus: A Practical Guide for Improving Communication and Getting What You Want in Your Relationships.* New York: HarperCollins.

Hacker, Andrew. 1997. *Money: Who Has How Much and Why.* New York: Scribner.

Hagan, John, and Fiona Kay. 1995. *Gender in Practice: A Study of Lawyers Lives.* New York: Oxford University Press.

Halbwachs, Maurice. [1941, 1952] 1992. *On Collective Memory,* ed. Lewis A. Coser. Chicago: Universiy of Chicago Press.

Hall, Oswald. 1946. "The Informal Organization of the Medical Profession." *Canadian Journal of Economics and Political Science* 12: 30–41.

Hays, Sharon. 1996. *The Cultural Contradictions of Motherhood.* New Haven: Yale University Press.

Heinz, John P., and Edward O. Laumann. 1982. *Chicago Lawyers: The Social Structure of the Bar.* New York: Russell Sage Foundation; Chicago: American Bar Association.

Hewlett, Sylvia Ann. 1986. *A Lesser Life: The Myth of Women's Liberation in America.* New York: W. Morrow.

Hochschild, Arlie Russell. 1979. "Emotion Work, Feeling Rules and Social Structure." *American Journal of Sociology* 85, 2 (November): 551–595.

————. 1989. *The Second Shift.* New York: Viking.

————. 1997. *The Time Bind: When Work Becomes Home and Home Becomes Work.* New York: Metropolitan Books.

Hoff, Joan. 1991. *Law, Gender, and Injustice: A Legal History of U.S. Women.* New York: New York University Press.

Hoffman, Paul. 1973. *Lions in the Streets.* New York: Signet.

Homans, George Caspar. 1950. *The Human Group.* New York: Harcourt, Brace.

————. 1961. *Social Behavior: Its Elementary Forms.* New York: Harcourt, Brace, and World.

Hughes, Everett. 1945. "Dilemmas and Contradictions of Status." *American Journal of Sociology* 50: 353–359.

Hunnicutt, Benjamin Kline. 1988. *Work Without End: Abandoning Shorter Hours from the Right Work.* Philadelphia: Temple University Press.

Ichniowski, Bernard E., and Anne E. Preston. 1986. "New Trends in Part-Time

Employment." In *Industrial Relations Research Association 38th Annual Proceedings,* 60–67.

Jacobs, Jerry, and Kathleen Gerson. 1997. "The Endless Day or the Flexible Office?" Report to the Alfred P. Sloan Foundation, June.

Jacobs, Jerry A., and Zhenchao Qian. 1997. "The Career Mobility of Part-Time Workers." In *Research in Social Stratification and Mobility,* vol. 15, 29–56, ed. Michael Wallace and Robert Althauser. JAI Press.

Jacobs, Jerry A., Marie Lukens, and Michael Useem. "Organizational, Job and Individual Determinants of Workplace Training: Evidence from the National Organizations Survey." Social Science Quarterly 77 (1): 159–176.

Kalleberg, Arne. 1995. "Symposium: Part-Time Work and Workers in the United States: Correlates and Policy Issues." *Washington and Lee Law Review* 52: 771–798.

Kamerman, Sheila B., and Alfred J. Kahn. 1981. *Child Care, Family Benefits and Working Parents: A Study in Comparative Policy.* New York: Columbia University.

Kanter, Rosabeth Moss. 1977. *Men and Women of the Corporation.* New York: Basic Books.

Kingston, Paul. 1990. "Illusions and Ignorance About the Family-Responsive Workplace." *Journal of Social Issues* 11:4 (December): 438–454.

Kirk, Margaret O. 1995. "The Temps in the Gray Flannel Suits." *New York Times,* Business Section, Sunday, Dec. 17, 13.

Klein, Chris. 1996. "Women's Progress Slows at Top Firms." *National Law Journal* (May 6).

Komarovsky, Mirra. 1946. "Cultural Contradictions and Sex Roles." *American Journal of Sociology* 52: 184–189.

Kronman, Anthony T. 1993. *The Lost Lawyer: Failing Ideals of the Legal Profession.* Cambridge, MA: Belknap Press of Harvard University Press.

Landers, Renee M., James Rebitzer, and Lowell Taylor. 1996. "Rat Race Redux: Adverse Selection in the Determination of Work Hours in Firms." *American Economic Review* (June): 329–348.

Leibowitz, Arleen, and Tollinson, Robert. 1980. "Free Riding, Shirking and Team Production in Legal Partnerships." *Economic Inquiry* 18: 380.

Levin, Jack, and William C. Levin. 1991. "Sociology of Educational Late Blooming." *Sociological Forum* 6 (4): 661–679.

Linowitz, Sol, with Martin Mayer. 1994. *The Betrayed Profession: Lawyering at the End of the Twentieth Century.* New York: Charles Scribner s Sons.

Lipset, Seymour Martin, Martin A. Trow, and James S. Coleman, with a foreword by Clark Kerr. 1962. *Union Democracy: The Internal Politics of the International Typographical Union.* Garden City, NY: Doubleday.

Lufkin, Martha. 1997. "Part-time Work's Around, But Few Do It." *National Law Journal* (Aug. 18): C5.

Lynd, Robert. 1939. *Knowledge for What?* Princeton: Princeton University Press.

Mack, Dana. 1997. *The Assault on Parenthood: How Our Culture Undermines the Family.* New York: Simon and Schuster.

Malinowski, Branislaw. 1932. *Crime and Custom in Savage Society.* London: Apul, Trench and Trubner.

Markus, Hazel Rose, Patricia R. Mullally, and Shinobu Kitayama. 1997. "Selfways: Diversity in Modes of Cultural Participation." In *The Conceptual Self in Context,* ed. Ulric Neisser and David A. Jopling. Cambridge and New York: Cambridge University Press.

McKenna, Elizabeth Perle. 1997. *When Work Doesn't Work Anymore: Women Work and Identity.* New York: Delacorte Press.

Melbin, Murray. 1987. *Night as Frontier: Colonizing the World After Dark.* New York: Free Press.

Merton, Robert. 1957. *Social Theory and Social Structure.* Glencoe, IL: Free Press.

————. 1976. *Sociological Ambivalence and Other Essays.* New York: Free Press.

————. 1984. "Socially Expected Durations: A Case Study of Concept Formation in Sociology." In *Conflict and Consensus: A Festschrift in Honor of Lewis A. Coser,* ed. Walter Powell and Richard Robbins, 262–286. New York: Free Press.

Merton, Robert, George G. Reader, and Patricia L. Kendall, eds. 1957. *The Student-Physician: Introductory Studies in the Sociology of Medical Education.* Cambridge: Published for the Commonwealth Fund by Harvard University Press.

Mirvis, Philip, and Douglas T. Hall. 1994. "Psychological Success and the Boudaryless Career." *Journal of Organizational Behavior* 15: 365–380.

Mizruchi, Ephraim H., Barry Glassner, and Thomas Pastorello. 1982. *Time and Aging.* Bayside, NY: General Hall.

Modell, John, Frank Furstenberg Jr., and Theodore Hershberg. 1978. "Social Change and Transitions to Adulthood in Historical Perspective." In *The American Family in Socio-Historical Perspective,* ed. Michael Gordon. New York: St. Martin's.

Morrill, Calvin. 1995. *The Executive Way.* Chicago: University of Chicago Press.

Murphree, Mary C. 1984. "Brave New Office: The Changing Role of the Legal Secretary." In *My Troubles Are Going to Have Trouble with Me: Everyday Trials and Triumphs of Women Workers,* ed. K. Sacks and D. Remy, 140-159. New Brunswick, NJ: Rutgers University Press.

Nelson, Robert L. 1988. *Partners with Power: The Social Transformation of the Large Law Firm.* Berkeley: University of California Press.

Neugarten, Bernice. 1979. "Time, Life and the Life Cycle." *American Journal of Psychiatry* 136: 887–893.

Newman, Katherine, 1993. *Declining Fortunes: The Withering of the American Dream.* New York: Basic Books.

Osterman, Paul, ed. 1996. *Broken Ladders: Managerial Careers in the New Economy.* New York: Oxford University Press.

Parcel, Toby L., and E.G. Menanghan. 1994. *Parents' Jobs and Children's Lives.* New York: Aldine.

Parsons, Talcott. [1939] 1954. "The Professions and Social Structure." In *Essays in Sociological Theory.* Glencoe, IL: Free Press.

Parsons, Talcott, and Edward A. Shils, eds. 1951. *Toward a General Theory of Action.* Cambridge: Harvard University Press.

Pavalko, Ronald. 1988. *Sociology of Occupations and Professions.* Itasca, IL: G.E. Peacock.

Potuchek, Jean L. 1997. *Who Supports the Family: Gender and Breadwinning in Dual-Career Marriages.* Stanford, CA: Stanford University Press.

Pound, Roscoe. 1909. "Etiquette of Justice." *Proceedings of the Nebraska State Bar Association* 3: 23–51.

Powell, Michael. 1988. *From Patrician to Professional Elite: The Transformation of the New York City Bar Association.* New York: Russell Sage Foundation.

Pristin, Terry. 1998. "The Newest Temps in Law Firms: Lawyers." *New York Times,* Feb. 24, B7.

Rebitzer, James B., and Lowell J. Taylor. 1995. "Do Labor Markets Provide Enough Short-hour Jobs? An Analysis of Work Hours and Work Incentives." *Economic Inquiry* 33: 257–273.

Rhode, Deborah. 1997. *Speaking of Sex: The Denial of Gender Inequality.* Cambridge: Harvard University Press.

Robinson, John P., and Geoffrey Godbey. 1997. *Time for Life.* University Park: Pennsylvania University Press.

Rogers, Jackie Krasas. n.d. "Lawyers for Rent: The Gendering of Temporary Employment for Lawyers." Unpublished paper, Department of Sociology, University of Southern California 90089-2539.

Roth, Julius A. 1963. *Timetables.* Indianapolis: Bobbs-Merrill.

Sassen, Saskia. 1991. *The Global City.* Princeton, NJ: Princeton University Press.

Scheff, Thomas. 1988. "Shame and Conformity: The Deference-Emotion System." *American Sociological Review* 53 (June): 395–406.

Schor, Juliet B. 1993. *The Overworked American: The Unexpected Decline of Leisure.* New York: Basic Books.

Schrank, Robert. 1978. *Ten Thousand Working Days.* Cambridge: MIT Press.

Schwab, Jolie. 1994. Report to the Committee on Women in the Profession. Unpublished paper.

Seron, Carroll. 1996. *The Business of Practicing Law: The Work Lives of Solo and Small-Firm Attorneys.* Philadelphia: Temple University Press.

Seron, Carroll, Martin Frankel, Douglas Muzzio, Joseph Pereria, and Gregg Van Ryzin. 1997. A Report of the Perceptions and Experiences of Lawyers, Judges, and Court Employees Concerning Gender, Racial, and Ethnic Fairness in the Federal Courts of the Second Circuit of the United States.

Shellenbarger, Sue. 1997. "These Top Bosses May Signal Move to More Family Time." *Wall Street Journal,* April 30, B1.

Skolnick, Arlene. 1991. *Embattled Paradise: The American Family in an Age of Uncertainty.* New York: Basic Books.

Smigel, Erwin O. 1964. *The Wall Street Lawyer: Professional Organization Man?* New York: Free Press.

Snider, Anna. 1998. "City Bar to Study Why Law Firms Lose Associates." *New York Law Journal* (Jan. 21): 1, 2.

Sorokin, Pitirim A., and Robert K. Merton. 1937. "Social Time: A Methodological and Functional Analysis." *American Journal of Sociology* 42: 615–629.

Spangler, Eve. 1986. *Lawyers for Hire: Salaried Professionals at Work*. New Haven: Yale University Press.

Tilly, Chris. 1990. *Short Hours, Short Shrift*. Washington, DC: Economic Policy Institute.

Trotter, Michael. 1997. *Profit and the Practice of Law*. Athens: University of Georgia Press.

U. S. Department of Labor. 1995. *Report on the American Workforce*. Washington, DC: U. S. Government Printing Office.

Ueda, Michael. 1998. "Legal Profs Debate Job Satisfaction." *San Francisco Daily Journal,* Jan. 23, 2.

West, Candice, and Don H. Zimmerman. 1987. "Doing Gender." *Gender and Society* (2): 125–152.

Whitehead, Barbara Dafoe. 1997. *The Divorce Culture*. New York: Knopf.

Whyte, William Foote. 1969. *Organizational Behavior: Theory and Application*. Homewood, IL: R.D. Irwin.

Wilkins, David R., and G. Mitu Gulati. 1996. "Why Are There So Few Black Lawyers in Corporate Law Firms?: An Institutional Analysis." *California Law Review* 84, 3 (May): 493–625.

Willis, Paul E. 1977. *Learning to Labour: How Working Class Kids Get Working Class Jobs*. Farnborough: Saxon House.

Wrigley, Julia. 1995. *Other People's Children*. New York: Basic Books.

Zelizer, Viviana A. 1994. *The Social Meaning of Money*. New York: Basic Books.

Zerubavel, Eviatar. 1981. *Hidden Rhythms: Schedules and Calendars in Social Life*. Chicago: University of Chicago Press.

Zuboff, Shoshana. 1988. *In the Age of the Smart Machine: The Future of Work and Power*. New York: Basic Books.

ENDNOTES

1. These cases represent real experiences but the names and their places of work have been changed. They are not those of particular individuals interviewed for our study.
2. The term "time deviant" has been conceptualized by Byrne (1988).
3. See also "Employment Trends, 1984–1996, reported by the NALP on its Web site, 1997.
4. A handful but growing number of firms and corporations use lawyers on a contract basis, as temporary workers. Men as well as women fall into this category; many are biding their time until they find permanent full-time jobs. These attorneys face problems that are somewhat different from the ones reported in this book but share some of the issues we discuss.
5. According to the U.S. Department of Labor's *Report on the American Workforce* (1995), the labor force participation rate of mothers of preschoolers alone (children under age six) rose from 39 percent in 1975 to 60.3 percent in 1994.
6. Balancing work and family is a regular topic of a column in the *Wall Street Journal* by Sue Shellenbarger entitled "Work and Family." She reported, for example (April 30, 1997, p. B1) that finding an appropriate balance is the leading source of workplace pressure for 74 percent of men and 78 percent of women surveyed by the American Society of Chartered Financial Consultants and the Ethics Officer Association. She notes that some of these "determined integrators of work and family are breaking into top management." Many social scientists agree that the problems of balancing work and family are no longer private troubles, but have become public concerns. However, they also agree that the social definition of the issue has changed far more than has institutional practice (Kingston, 1990).
   Furthermore, general dissatisfaction with the legal profession, partly a result of long hours and boredom, was reported by 20 percent of young lawyers, according to a national survey of 1,000 lawyers conducted by the *National Law Journal* in 1990. Fifteen percent of women expressed the same discontents as well as 32 percent of black American lawyers (Epstein, [1981] 1993, p. 447). The National Survey of Lawyers' Career Satisfaction (American Bar Association [1990: 52] showed that job satisfaction fell 5 percent for men between 1984 and 1990 despite rising incomes (Hirsch, 1992).
7. We note that this study is of voluntary part-time lawyers in contrast to those who can only find part-time work because of a lack of employment opportunities. In that respect, the part-time work of our sample is a deviant case since most part-time workers engage in it involuntarily (Jacobs and Qian, 1995; Tilly, 1990; Ichniowski and Preston, 1986; Blank, 1990. This is true for professionals as well as other workers, according to Challenger, Gray, & Christmas, an outplacement firm in Chicago (*New York Times*, Dec. 17, 1995, p. 13).

8. See for example, Galanter and Palay, 1991.
9. Beechey and Perkins (1987) found that regardless of their jobs, women part-time workers are always defined as marginal workers.
10. According to the sociologist Arne Kalleberg (1995) part-time workers and full-time workers do not differ much in their attitudes toward work. All workers value interesting work that provides opportunity for advancement and gives them security (pp. 777–778).
11. See Rogers (n.d.), who, in her study of contract (*i.e.,* temporary) lawyers, conceptualized their status as a "stigmatized identity" (p. 1).
12. *E.g.,* Galanter and Paley, 1991; Heinz and Laumann, 1982; Spangler, 1986.
13. See *e.g.,* Hochschild, 1997; Kirk, 1995; Schwab, 1994.
14. Even today, our recent study of glass ceilings in large corporate law firms (Epstein *et al.,* 1995) reports, 40 percent of male partners in large law firms have wives who are not employed. Most of the male partners are 40 to 70. Only 11 percent of lawyers 40 years of age and above are women (Curran and Carson, 1994). Also see Seron (1996) for a very similar pattern among solo and small-firm attorneys.
15. This figure comes from a survey of the 250 largest law firms in the United States conducted by the *National Law Journal* (Klein, 1996).
16. Women who followed a traditional route toward promotion (entering a firm from law school and moving toward partnership) had an even smaller chance for promotion than they had in the early 1980s. Thus, associates who were hired starting in 1982 and who could be expected to make partner around 1990 found competition becoming more intense as they approached the moment of decision. Male associates hired between the years 1973 and 1981 had a mean rate of promotion to partner of 21.5 percent. Women associates hired in the same period had a mean rate of promotion of 15.25 percent (Epstein *et al.,* 1995, pp.358–359). Further, among the post-1981 cohorts, women faced a disproportionately smaller chance of making partner (*ibid.*).
17. The sector of the profession with the least sex imbalance is "legal aid/public defender," where women make up 38 percent of lawyers. Women attorneys represent 26 percent of those who teach law (Curran and Carson, 1994).
18. A number of Supreme Court decisions have made this much more difficult, however. For example, in *Hishon v. King and Spalding* (467 U.S. 69 [1984]), the Supreme Court held that under Title VII of the Civil Rights Act of 1964, law firms may not discriminate on the basis of sex in regard to partnership promotions. The Supreme Court ruled in *Price Waterhouse v. Hopkins* (109 S. St. 1775 [1989]) that in some cases alleging intentional discrimination, employers have the burden of proving their refusal to hire or promote is based on legitimate and not discriminatory reasons (Hoff, 1991, pp. 402, 406).
19. Our findings suggest that this pattern is much more typical than earlier studies of career patterns of lawyers might suggest (see especially Heinz and Laumann, 1982), which showed that private, large firm, and government attorneys work in separate "hemispheres" with little movement between and across these arenas of work. The disproportionately large presence of women in government suggests that the source and pattern of this career track requires further and systematic study.

20. Coser defines greedy institutions as those "which make total claims of their members...[and] seek exclusive and undivided loyalty and attempt to reduce their claims of competing roles and status positions on those they wish to encompass within their borders" (p. 5).

21. The very notion of a professional career is marked by temporal sequences. Robert Merton labels these as "status sequences" (1957). See Chapter 7 on mobility.

22. This is consistent with the sociologist Andrew Abbot's (1989b) point that over the course of the twentieth century, occupational solidarity has been replaced by organizational loyalty.

23. See Landers, Rebitzer, and Taylor (1996), p. 216.

24. Landers, Rebitzer, and Taylor (1996) report that aggregate statistics show that the work hours of college-educated employees have been rising steadily since the 1940s, and there is little evidence that "short-hour" jobs (*i.e.,* less than the standard number of hours expected in any realm of work) are appearing in professional firms (p. 215).

25. In 1938 the Roosevelt administration passed the Fair Labor Standards Act mandating minimum wages and set the workweek at 40 hours (starting in 1941). Hours worked above 40 are to be compensated at a rate of time-and-a-half. Executive, managerial, and professional employees are exempt from both minimum wage and overtime pay provisions (Bremner, 1985, pp. 81–82).

   By 1920 most organized labor had won the eight-hour day, and by the end of that decade the five-day workweek was widespread in certain industries, such as clothing manufacturing. In 1929, 400,000 to 500,000 employees worked a five-day week. The trend toward shorter hours reversed during the Depression, when as employment decreased, hours worked per employee increased (Hunnicutt, 1988, pp. 70–71). According to Card and Krueger (1995, p. 238), in 1998, 87.7 percent of workers nationwide were covered by the act.

26. The relationship between hours worked and potential for promotion is analyzed by Landers, Rebitzer, and Taylor (1996).

27. For example, most graduates of elite national law schools find jobs in these firms after law school. In addition, studies show (Epstein *et al.,* 1995; Granfield, 1992) that lawyers who leave or expect to leave large firms regard their time there as training providing a standard of excellence for work in other sectors of the law such as government and corporate legal departments.

28. In large law firms reports of 60- or 70-hour workweeks were not uncommon, and many attorneys work on weekends and holidays regularly (Epstein *et al.,* 1995).

29. Such as those noted in the novels of Louis Auchincloss, *e.g., The Great World and Timothy Colt* (1956), and *The Partners* (1974); see also Smigel (1964) and Epstein ([1981] 1993) for anecdotes about marathon work assignments in large firms.

30. As an indicator of this, in February 1997 Dean Paul Brest of Stanford Law School and the deans of other prominent law schools met with partners from distinguished large corporate law firms to explore the changing ethos of the legal profession and the changing role of lawyers.

31. Goffman (1959) contends that people tend to play parts, behaving in such ways to convince others that they possess the particular attributes desired.

32. As Abbott (1989a) and other scholars of the professions define them, professions "are exclusive groups applying somewhat abstract knowledge to particular cases" (p. 8). See also A.M. Carr-Saunders and P.A.Wilson, 1933a, Talcott Parsons [1939] 1954.

33. Indicative of this trend is a feature that runs on the front page of the "B" section of *The National Law Journal*. Titled "In-House Counsel," the column profiles a general counsel of a major corporation who almost invariably emphasizes pride in reducing outside counsel billings. For a discussion of the increasingly competitive nature of large-firm practice, see Galanter and Palay (1991).

34. The monitoring of hours is growing more intense in other professions, such as medicine with the advent of managed health care organizations. It is part of what D. Collinson and M. Collinson (1997) call "time-space surveillance," based on their work in industry showing that managers are increasingly evaluated on their time management and workplace presence. These authors point out that manual labor has always been controlled and that time discipline is central to managers' exercise of control but that managers themselves are manipulated by time (and space) surveillance (p. 386).

35. Many men are able to perform according to "macho" standards only because women's labor in the home frees them to do so. In the Epstein *et al.* study of large corporate law firms, 40 percent of male partners had wives who were not employed outside the home. See also Collinson and Collinson (1997) and Buswell and Jenkins (1994), who suggest that the current speeding-up of practices is primarily accomplished by men who are "using the fuel of women's time" (p. 89, as cited in Collinson and Collinson, p. 384).

36. See also Sebastian deGrazia (1962), and William J. Goode (1979).

37. Goffman writes "an attribute that stigmatizes one type of possessor can confirm the usualness of another, and therefore is neither creditable nor discreditable as a thing in itself" (p. 3).

38. The stigma attached to the contract lawyers nay be the worst; in any case it is widely acknowledged. A *New York Times* article (Kirk, 1995) quoted a contract lawyer, "There is sometimes a stigma attached to being a contract attorney" (p. 13). However, there is a growing use of temporary lawyers, about 30 percent a year, according to *The New York Times* (Pristin, 1998), with New York the largest market. Some firms use them for special projects—*e.g.,* White and Case, a large New York firm, hired 100 to work on an antitrust case—but lawyers from other firms interviewed for the article voiced concern about the quality of temporary contract lawyers.

39. As Goffman (1963) writes, "Because of the great rewards in being considered normal, almost all persons who are in a position to pass will do so on some occasion" (p. 74).

40. Rogers (n.d.) reports that contract lawyers are paid far below the hourly rates of regular lawyers. In California the pay rates are between $35 and $55 an hour but can be as low as $25 or as high as $100. But clients are billed between $100 and $300 an hour for their services (p. 10).

41. For workers in general, on an hourly basis part-time workers earn less than full-time workers. In addition to lower wages, part-time work also results in the loss of

benefits, job security, and chances for training and advancement (Gornick and Jacobs, 1996).

42. The incomes of lawyers in this study are reported in Table 6.1 in Appendix C.

43. See Table 6.2 in Appendix C.

44. According to Gabriel (1997), "Insults include behavior or discourse, oral or written, which is perceived, experienced, constructed, and at times intended as slighting, humiliating, or offensive.... Insults are also a fairly regular phenomenon of organizational life (p. 4).

45. Modell, Furstenberg, and Hershberg (1978) claim, for example, that growing up in 19th-century America was characterized by individual variation and choice rather than by tightly defined stages.

46. See Landers, Rebitzer, and Taylor (1996) for an analysis of the pressures on associates to work long hours and the perception of managing partners and associates that hours are an indicator of hard-to-measure characteristics such as commitment or ambition (p. 329).

47. Part-time workers, as a general pattern, typically lose career advancement opportunities and receive less on-the-job training in all sectors of the economy and throughout the world, although the degree of disadvantage varies. See Gornick and Jacobs (1996); Tilly (1990).

48. "Part-timers give up mobility," said Wendy Leibowitz, a writer for *American Lawyer* who reported on her study of 15 lawyers and 20 full-time administrators in large firms (Feb. 13, 1995) at a meeting of the part-time lawyers' network (LAAWS) of the Association of the Bar of the City of New York. "Many say it does not work," she noted.

49. The firm with three part-time partners was different from most others in that it had a "lock-step" compensation system (making it possible to calculate a distinct percentage for the three partners, who worked between 80 and 90 percent time). Yet, we learned that the biographies and the circumstances of the part-time partners were quite different from each other, attesting to the fact that there is no established track for part-time attorneys to achieve partnership in that firm.

50. A number of lawyers we interviewed who participated in the Association of the Bar of the City of New York LAAWS Network had been laid off from their jobs while working part-time schedules.

51. See *Wall Street Journal* (May 19, 1997), p. B1.

52. See Landers, Rebitzer, and Taylor (1996), p. 330.

53. Non-equity status is growing in law firms, according to a survey conducted by the *National Law Journal* (France, 1994). Of the 250 largest firms in the country, those reporting non-equity partners rose to 124 from 111 in 1993. But the *Journal* reports that firms make only limited disclosure—or none at all—about non-equity partners, fearing that clients will learn their status and interpret the title as a badge of inferiority.

54. Pp. 415–416.

55. A discussion of the functions of "schmoozing" may be found in Robert Schrank's (1978) account of workplace experiences.

56. The norms of proper timing are suggested by Sorokin and Merton's (1937) early analysis, later summarized by Roth (1963) in his concept of "career timetables."

57. See also footnote for percentages of lawyers taking part-time schedules in other large cities.

58. There is a broad sociological literature on the social consequences of differences in expectations and rank in the various statuses people hold in their "status-sets" (Merton, 1957). Everett Hughes (1945) devoted attention to the discomfort experienced by individuals who hold such discrepant statuses as woman and engineer, black and physician, because of the inappropriate responses of role partners who become confused about how to react to people who (for example) command respect in one status, but who hold a subordinate rank by virtue of holding another. (The title of this section is the title of Hughes's essay on this matter.) His work illustrated a research agenda regarding the dynamics of status-sets (Merton, 1957), and it inspired research by Komarovsky (1946) and Epstein (1970, 1988).

59. Exceptions, of course, are the titles of "special counsel" or "of counsel" in private firms, traditionally held by part-time (male) lawyers close to retirement, or by full-time lawyers who remain in firms without partnership. Nearly half of the part-time attorneys from law firms in this study reported that they hoped to ask their firms to make them of counsel or had already made the request and were denied.

60. While some government and corporation attorneys also expressed frustration about the lack of official recognition accorded to them as part-timers, status discrepancies are probably not as obvious in these sectors as they are in private law firms. Given the "up and out" system which makes room for new recruits in private law firms, there is a continual influx of newly minted lawyers. This contributes to an age and experience discrepancy that tends to be more pronounced than in government agencies and corporations, where turnover is not built into the structure of the organization.

61. Markus and her associates (1997) point out that "Particularized senses of the self—self-concepts and individual identities—are always grounded in the complex of consensual understandings and customary behavioral routines relevant to being a self in a given sociocultural and historical context" (p. 15).

62. There is a large literature on exchange analysis, and the common thread that runs through it is the importance of mutuality between the members of a social system or group. Violation of mutuality is regarded as exploitation by the group or subgroup that gets more than they return to the other (by whatever means the calculus is made). Gouldner (1960) in writing of the ubiquity of the value of reciprocity cites Parsons and Shils (eds.) (1951), who contended that if a social system is to be stable, there must be some "mutuality of gratification." Social systems, therefore, presumably depend in part on the mutually contingent exchange of gratifications, that is, on reciprocity of exchange (p. 128). Gouldner also cites Malinowski (1932), who wrote that reciprocity entails a "mutual dependence and [is] realized in the equivalent arrangement of reciprocal services." Reciprocity is the "pattern of exchange through which the mutual dependence of people, brought about by the division of labor, is realized." It is to be noted that reciprocity is not the exchange of the same good or behavior but something regarded as equivalent.

63. "Up or out" refers to the fact that in private law firms associates typically are made partners after a prescribed number of years or are expected to find work elsewhere

(Epstein *et al.,* 1995), much the same as in academic life where professors who are denied tenure are expected to leave the institution and find work elsewhere.

64. "Professional socialization" has been identified as the process by which neophytes in a profession become imbued with the values and norms that define it. Thus, they internalize a "professional identity" that orients them to standards of behavior. See Freidson (1986), Goode (1957), Merton, Reader, and Kendall (1957), and Parsons [1939] 1954.

65. Such as helping a colleague with a nonwork-related problem, sharing professional gossip, or engaging in small talk (see Epstein, 1991).

66. For example, Robert Lynd, in *Knowledge for What?* (1939), points out that Americans believed that "all men are equal" but that "people get what they deserve."

67. A special issue of *Business Week* (April 21, 1997) ran a cover story entitled "Executive Pay: It's Out of Control" and reported that top American CEOs had an average pay raise of 54 percent and factory workers 3 percent in the past year (p. 59). The rationale that the high rates for executives were based on performance criteria was challenged by Warren Bennis, distinguished professor of business administration at the University of Southern California, who was quoted as saying performance targets are often set so low—or so loosely—that they're virtually meaningless. "Performance criteria are almost like intellectual silly putty" (p. 62).

68. The classic functional analysis of the stratification system, "Some Principles of Stratification" by Kingsley Davis and Wilbert Moore (1945), sought to explain the high pay of professionals contrasted with other workers by the high investments they had made in preparation and training and the fact that their services could not be reproduced by others with less training.

69. See George Homans (1961) on justice in the social group.

70. See Chapter 6.

71. Some of these are described in Chapter 1.

72. In 1993, 58 percent of women with children under six worked in the labor force, an increase from 12 percent in 1950 (Hays, 1996, pp. 3–4).

73. *Family in America,* 1, Rockford Institute, Center for the Family in America, November 1987, p. 1.

74. *Family in America,* 2, Rockford Institute, Center for the Family in America, May 1988, p. 3.

75. See, for example, an article in the *New York Daily News,* "Nanny in Tot Sex Horror: Dad Catches Her in Act on Hidden Camera" (1998, p. 7) and an accompanying piece "Spying on the Sitter" (Hutchinson, 1998, p. 7).

76. The recently enacted welfare reform legislation, called the "Personal Responsibility and Work Opportunity Reconciliation Act" of 1996, mandates that women with children over the age of five seek paid employment or eventually lose their benefits. At the same time, leading political and moral entrepreneurs, especially from the religious right, are raising questions about the negative consequences women's employment has on the family and particularly on the well-being of children. See, for example, the work of the Rockford Institute on the Family Research Council.

77. As do most working families. See Sheila Kamerman and Alfred Kahn (1981).
78. For a discussion of the symbiotic relationship between high-income professionals and low-wage and immigrant service providers see Sassen (1991). Of course, male professionals have long depended on the service provided by wives.
79. According to Roscoe Pond (1909), a profession "refers to a group...pursuing a learned art as a common calling in the spirit of public service—no less a public service because it may incidentally be a means of livelihood."
80. The sociologist Scott Coltrane (1996, p. 70) noted a similar phenomenon in families where spouses consciously decided to share housework. In a study of 20 families, 11 had a wife who worked part-time. In only one of the 11 did husbands contribute equally to cooking and cleaning. Among the nine families where both partners worked full-time, eight of nine did so.
81. For a discussion of the symbolic meaning of money for American women in the 20th century, see Zelizer (1994).
82. The data in this chapter are based on responses from 62 attorneys. Eighty-eight respondents were asked to complete a form at the conclusion of their interview and to return the questionnaire in a stamped, addressed envelope; of these, 62 returned the questionnaire, for a response rate of 70 percent. Please note that the remainder of the part-time lawyers were drawn from a study conducted by Epstein *et al.* (1995).
83. We witnessed attorneys' conference calls in action at home during interviews, sometimes with babies in the next room.
84. Among attorneys in large firms, 73 percent reported that they had a fax machine; among in-house attorneys, 64 percent reported a fax machine at home.
85. As we noted earlier, the tiny number of minority lawyers may result from their low representation in the profession (Wilkins and Gulati, 1996), and also from the fact that minority lawyers are less likely to be able to forgo a full-time salary, perhaps because they feel their positions are more tenuous than white lawyers". Aggregate figures show that while 18.8 percent of white workers work part-time, only 15.1 percent of black workers do, and while 28.3 percent of white women work part-time, only 18.5 percent of black women workers do (*Employment & Earnings,* Bureau of Labor Statistics, 1997, Table 8).

INDEX